*Reinterpreting the
New Testament*

Robert M. Price

REINTERPRETING THE NEW TESTAMENT

*Don't Be So Sure You Know
What it Means!*

TIMAIOS PRESS

These essays by Robert McNair Price (born 1954) were originally published as follows: "A Political Jesus?" in *Christian*New Age Quarterly* vol. 23, #4 (Autumn 2018); "Apocryphal Addenda: More Lost Gospel Novels" in *Journal of Higher Criticism* vol. 13, #2, 2018; "Did Paul Think of the Pre-Incarnate Christ as God?" in *Patreon* post March 23, 2018; "Skepticism and Historical Method" as a lecture given at Skepticon 2 Redux, 2009; "The Austerity Gospel of Gordon Fee" in *JHC* vol. 14, #1, 2019; "The Synoptic Apocalypse and the Son of Man" in *JHC* vol. 15, #1, 2020; "The Retreat from Radical Prayer" in *JHC* vol. 14, #2, 2019; "The Theological Tragedy of George Eldon Ladd" in *American Rationalist* 61, No. 5 (Sept./Oct. 2015); "Toward a Legalistic Understanding of the Sermon on the Mount" in *JHC* vol. 13, #4, 2018; "Was There a Historical Apollonius of Tyana?" in *JHC* vol. 13, #1, 2018; "William Lane Craig: Scholar or Apologist?" as an Opening Statement for Debate with William Lane Craig, 1999.

EDITOR:
Rickard Berghorn.
Author, literary historian, publisher, and student of
history of science and ideas.

COVER:
Photoshoped part of "The Triumph
of Christianity over Paganism," painting
by Gustave Doré (1832-83).

Timaios Press, Sweden.
www.timaiospress.com
Imprint of Aleph Bokförlag.

Printed and distributed by Ingram
Content Group LLC in La Vergne, TN, USA.

First edition (hardback), March 2020.
This is the second edition (paperback), March 2020.

ISBN 978-91-87611-31-5

Contents

A Political Jesus?

Traditionally it has not been supposed that Jesus had anything quite like what we would call political opinions or beliefs. Orthodox Christians in fact did not picture Jesus as having any *opinions* on anything at all. You know the slogan: "The gospel is good *news*, not good *views*." Even so, as the earthly avatar of Jehovah, Jesus did not need "opinions," which are, by definition, less than certain, more tentative, like theories which compete with rival theories. What need had he for such gropings? After all, he did not see in a glass darkly but already face to face. And this contrast hints at a serious inconsistency underlying the whole endeavor to reconstruct "the politics of Jesus." On the one hand, we ask what this *man's* political opinions might be, as if we were asking after those of Ashley Judd or Sean Penn. On the other, we ask this because we imagine that, whatever views we may decide Jesus held, they will be normative for us, implying we consider them no mere opinions from which we may learn, but rather divine dictates which we may demand that others must join us in following. It is a case of theo-political bait-and-switch and, finally, of cynical manipulation.

APOLITICAL APOCALYPSE

Some modern-era scholars have seen nothing political in Jesus as recorded in the gospels. This might be a good or a bad thing depending on how one looked at it. Rabbi Joseph Klausner,[1] generally an admirer of Jesus, regarded it as a regrettable blind spot that Jesus had nothing to say about political things, as he thus created a vacuum for the Christian Church which, having no guidance from him, defaulted into worldly politics, for instance, Caesaro-papist authoritarianism. Jesus

---

1 Joseph Klausner, *Jesus of Nazareth: His Life, Times, and Teaching* (New York: Macmillan, 1925).

could have prevented such abuses had he only done what Moses and Samuel and Chairman Mao did. But instead, he shrugged off any such duties: "O man, who appointed me a judge or an arbiter over you?" (Luke 12:13-14).

Liberal Protestant theologian Adolf Harnack[1] took a different view of the matter. Yes, Jesus had nothing to say on governance and policy, but that is good. Had he worked out some political theory or platform, it must soon become obsolete and incompatible as times and conditions changed. So he left that task to future generations, like the king who departed for a journey, entrusting money to his servants to see what they would do with it in his absence. (Compare Matthew 25:14-30 with 1 Corinthians 3:10-15.) It might be thought that Harnack forgot what he had said when he began to advocate the Social Gospel of humanitarian service in the name of Jesus, but I think it was rather that he took on that responsibility that Jesus had bequeathed to future generations of disciples, and he considered the Social Gospel to be the appropriate Christian response to the conditions of his age.

Albert Schweitzer[2] saw Jesus as providing no political guidance, but for almost the opposite reason that Harnack had suggested. Jesus

---

1 Adolf Harnack, *What Is Christianity?* Trans. Thomas Bailey Saunders (New York: Harper & Row, 1957), p. 119; Harnack, "The Evangelical Social Mission in Light of the History of the Church," Chapter I., "General Attitude of the Gospel towards Social Arrangements," in Adolf Harnack and Wilhelm Herrmann, *Essays on the Social Gospel.* Trans. G.M. Craig. Crown Theological Library Vol. XVIII (London: Williams & Norgate, 1907), pp. 13-14.

2 Albert Schweitzer, *The Quest of the Historical Jesus: A Critical Study of its Progress from Reimarus to Wrede.* Trans. W. Montgomery (New York: Macmillan, 1961). Otherwise, Schweitzer shared a good bit of agreement with Harnack: he approved the general, liberal ethical stance Harnack derived from Jesus as a model for us, but he thought Harnack mistaken in ascribing it directly to Jesus. Schweitzer saw Jesus' own ethics, the "interim ethic," as more radical in both motive and application. He also agreed with Harnack that Jesus gave no thought to social reform, caring only for individual piety.

did not trust Christians to deal in their best Christian way with the circumstances of their future because he believed there would *be* no future. The world as we know it would soon come crashing down at the blast of the Last Trumpet and the shout of the Archangel. Politics? Why bother rearranging the deck chairs on the Titanic? Any ethic must, given these constraints, be an *interim ethic*: emergency measures on the eve of the End. Extra righteousness, like turning the other cheek, or giving away your money to do the only thing left to be done with it: feeding those in imminent danger of starvation. On the one hand, you can afford to do it because there is no future to prudently provide for. On the other, you had best beef up your resume of good works because God will be checking it very soon. He's going to find out who's been naughty or nice!

SON OF MAN WITH A PLAN

There are, however, plenty of scholars who are confident Jesus was a political figure—and that they have his political leanings pretty well pegged. I will summarize what I would consider the main positions, evaluating them as I go.

Was Jesus a violent revolutionist? I believe the first to propose this was the eighteenth-century Deist Hermann Samuel Reimarus.[1] He noted that the gospels clearly depict Jesus' disciples expecting an earthly regime to be headed by their Master. They jockeyed for positions of honor and power alongside him. They expected the liberation of Israel from Roman rule (Luke 24:21; Acts 1:6). We also read that Jesus sent out his disciples, already in the days of his public ministry (Mark 6:7-13), to preach the coming of the kingdom of God, and we cannot imagine he would not have drilled them on what they were to preach, to make sure they were correctly representing him (cf. 1 John 2:19). If subsequent to this we see the disciples continuing in their belief in a this-worldly regime for Jesus and themselves as his cronies, we have no right to believe Jesus taught anything different, i.e., some more "spiri-

---

1 Charles H. Talbert, ed., *Reimarus: Fragments*. Trans. Ralph S. Fraser. Lives of Jesus Series (Philadelphia: Fortress Press, 1970).

tual" version of the coming kingdom (contra John 18:36). But Jesus' planned revolution failed, and the disciples regrouped, transforming Christianity from a political movement to an otherworldly salvation cult.

Decades later, Robert Eisler[1] renewed this theory, appealing to the then-recently discovered Slavonic version of Josephus' *Jewish War*, which contains a longer version of the notorious *Testimonium Flavianum* which occurs instead in Josephus' other major Greek language book, *Jewish Antiquities*, in shorter compass. (This would be just one of many parallel passages shared by both the *Antiquities* and the *Jewish War*.) In it, as Eisler translated the Slavonic text, Jesus is depicted as a revolutionary leader who justified Pilate's placard inscription, "Jesus of Nazareth, the man who would be king."

An even stronger version of this "Zealot hypothesis" was set forth by S.G.F. Brandon in a pair of books, *The Fall of Jerusalem and the Christian Church* (1951)[2] and *Jesus and the Zealots* (1967).[3] Zeroing in on a number of puzzling features of the gospel texts, Brandon said they make the most natural sense as loose ends that escaped the attention of the gospel writers as they sought to rewrite the history of Jesus. Let's take a brief look at some of the main ones.

The names and epithets of some of the disciples must give us pause. There is, of course, Simon Zelotes, i.e., Simon the Zealot, as modern translators render it. Granted, "the Zealot" might denote simply extraordinary piety, great religious zeal. But what might mark him out as exceptionally religious (i.e., fanatical) among a group of men who had abandoned home and family to follow a traveling guru, learning

1 Robert Eisler, *The Messiah Jesus and John the Baptist*. Trans. Alexander Haggerty Krappe (New York: Dial Press, 1931).

2 S.G.F. Brandon, *The Fall of Jerusalem and the Christian Church* (London: SPCK, 1951).

3 S.G.F. Brandon, *Jesus and the Zealots: A Study of the Political Factor in Primitive Christianity* (New York: Scribners, 1967). I am leaving out of consideration Reza Aslan's sorry book, *Zealot: The Life and Times of Jesus of Nazareth* (New York: Random House, 2013), as it is completely derivative of Brandon but gives him virtually no acknowledgement.

the arts of soapbox preaching and casting out demons? Wouldn't you say *all* these fellows qualified as "zealots"?

So what *else* might "the Zealot" have meant? During the Roman siege of Jerusalem a group of revolutionist *lestai* ("bandits") played a major role. While the group's name was a recent coinage, it represented the proud legacy of Judas the Galilean who had fomented the tax revolt against Rome in 6 C.E. They were in effect a new Hasmonean dynasty of freedom fighters. And, who knows? Perhaps the Zealot tag went back some years earlier. Or maybe tradition merely tagged Simon retrospectively with the slightly later term for revolutionaries. The punch line: one of Jesus' inner circle may have been a freedom-fighter.

Maybe not just one! Judas is dubbed "Iscariot." What does that mean? There are a hand full of possibilities, but probably the most popular among scholars is that "Iscariot" represents another revolutionist label, the *Sicarii*, or "dagger men," assassins who would slither through the crowds surrounding Roman officials and wealthy Jewish collaborators, short-swords up their sleeves, stab the victim, then join in the shouting while they slipped away undiscovered. Judas, then, may well be portrayed as another Zealot, "Judas the Sicarius."

Simon Peter is at one point (Matt. 16:17) called "Simon Bar-Jona," but this was not a typical Jewish patronymic (an epithet identifying you as So-and-so's son). Perhaps it originally denoted something else. There was another militant sect in New Testament times called the *Barjonim*, which means "the Terrorists,"[1] "the Extremists," "the Outlaws."[2] Was Peter a member?

If three of the twelve look like Zealots, it would hardly be a surprise if the rest were, too. And what does that imply about Jesus? You know, don't you?

Brandon did not mean that the evangelist Mark wanted readers to understand the names this way, only that he (or a predecessor) had suppressed the original meanings as part of a larger program of trying

---

1 Oscar Cullmann, *Jesus and the Revolutionaries*. Trans. Gareth Putnam (New York: Harper & Row, 1970), p. 63.

2 Eisler, pp. 252-253.

to shed and conceal the revolutionary origins of their religion. Another device for the same purpose was to shift the blame for Jesus' death from the Romans onto the Jews. Romans crucified seditionists; Jews (if they obtained Roman permission) stoned blasphemers. The role of the Jewish authorities in engineering Jesus' death has been enlarged: why? Because, Brandon suggests, Christians wanted to avert Roman suspicion from themselves by scape-goating the Jews, an easy target since Roman anti-Semitism increased every time there was a Jewish revolt.

James Valliant and Warren Fahy,[1] based on hitherto-neglected numismatic evidence, have strengthened Brandon's model, suggesting that the Roman-friendly Jesus of the canonical gospels represents a thoroughly Romanized version of the new faith redesigned to domesticate formerly seditionist Jesus-messianism. The basic difference is that, whereas Brandon inferred that Christians bowdlerized the Jesus story to cover their posteriors, Valliant and Fahy quite reasonably credit the project to Imperial (Flavian) sponsorship.[2]

As for the incompletely erased remnants of the original, revolutionary Christianity, they are both minor and major. Have you ever wondered what Jesus intended by saying, "The kingdom of God advances by violence, and violent men seize it by force" (Matt. 11:12; Luke 16:16)? I think Brandon is correct: the only likely sense to be made of it is as a reference to the insurrectionist violence of the Zealots. And it doesn't sound like any sort of a criticism.

And what did Jesus mean in Luke 22:36-37? "Let him who has no sword sell his cloak and buy one"? I'm guessing that the evangelist means to portray Jesus as setting the stage for the upcoming scene in the Garden of Gethsemane, where the disciples are to mount a token resistance to his arrest just so Isaiah 53:12 can be checked off the prophetic "To Do" list. Such a contrivance is fiction, not history. It is like

---

1 James S. Valliant and Warren Fahy, *Creating Christ: How Roman Emperors Created Christianity* (Crossroad Press, 2018).

2 A very similar case had been made a bit earlier by Joseph Atwill in his *Caesar's Messiah: The Roman Conspiracy to Invent Jesus* (Berkeley: Ulysses Press, 2005).

Jim Phelps setting up some scam on *Mission Impossible*. Why cook up such nonsense? To substitute for an original account in which Jesus told them to arm themselves in order to fend off an anticipated ambush, which is of course exactly what happens in the Gethsemane scene. Only originally they weren't just kidding around.

But the most striking piece of evidence for a now-hidden militant Jesus must be the so-called Cleansing of the Temple. Mark seems to want to depict the event as if Jesus had merely burst into a church basement rummage sale, upsetting some card tables piled with old Readers Digest books. Did he know (or did he want his readers to know) that the Court of the Gentiles, containing the livestock stalls and coin exchange tables, was actually *ten acres* in size? And Jesus is said to have seized control of the whole space, since he was able to prevent anyone carrying sacrificial vessels through the area (Mark 11:16). And how could he have done that unless he had brought a large contingent of armed men with him? Now the whole thing might be pure fiction; that's entirely possible. But if there was any factual basis to it, Mark has suppressed the scale and the stakes of the scene. Remember how Mark notes in passing that Barabbas was to be executed for his role in "the insurrection"? *What* insurrection? Why, the one Jesus had provoked in the Temple only brief hours before.

I'll tell you the truth: if there was a historical Jesus at all, this one's got my vote. But it remains altogether speculative, as all these theories must be. Let's try to keep that in mind as we proceed.

PRINCE OF PEACE

To go to the opposite extreme, might Jesus have been a *pacifist*, as Mennonites and Quakers think? This estimate of Jesus seems to be based upon a couple of gospel passages. The first is the famous command to turn the other cheek to get slapped after having the first one smacked (Matt. 5:39). The second is like unto it: Matthew 26:52, "All who take up the sword shall perish by the sword." Remarkably slim pickin's, no? The first passage concerns non-retaliation in interpersonal relations. Nothing at all is said of warfare. To count it as a proof text for pacifism is a pretty risky inference. If I were faced with the choice of meekly yielding to some terrorist versus defending myself with counter-violence, I think the mere *possibility* that Jesus meant to forbid self-defense would not be enough to tip the balance. I'd like better exegetical odds. How about you?

What Jesus says to Peter about the inevitable violent death of the violent man does not entirely fit the context. It is not exactly a command to renounce violence but more like a fatalistic observation like these. "The poor you have with you always" (Mark 14:7). "To him who has more, more will be given; from him who has nothing, what pittance he has will be taken away" (Matt. 25:29; Luke 19:26). "Take no thought for the morrow; today's troubles are enough for today" (Matt. 6:34). Or think of what Jesus says about divorce: it is always a declension from God's best plan, but Jesus says not a thing about henceforth prohibiting divorce, only that even God must reckon with the stubbornness of the human heart (Mark 10:5; cf., Gen. 8:21).

I watch reruns of *The Rifleman* pretty much every day. A recurring theme is that if a man acquires a reputation as a fast gun, he will forever be plagued by challengers hoping to outdraw him and to enhance their own reputations. The only way to escape this fate is to be outgunned—killed. "Those who live by the sword will sooner or later die the same way."

It is conceivable that Jesus shared the provisional quietism of the Dead Sea Scrolls sect. They would not indulge in violence against the enemies of the Jews. "Vengeance is mine! I will repay" (Rom. 12:19). They waited with growing impatience for God to open the skies and dispatch an army of angels to deal with the pagans. But when that day arrived, the sectarians would plunge right in with sword and shield. They even had battle plans drawn up! You can read them in the War Scroll ("The War of the Sons of Light and the Sons of Darkness"). Is this really pacifism?

A variation of the pacifist Jesus understands him as something of an accommodationist. That was the position of most Pharisees and of the Sadducees. They figured it would be suicide to take up arms in a war they could not win, so they swallowed hard and cooperated as best they could with Rome. This is the issue when Jesus' critics think to trap him with a question about Roman taxes. If Jews cough up the tax (and they'll be in big trouble if they don't), are they flouting the Torah? Uh, how would they be doing *that*?

Hadn't Jews long been paying taxes to foreign overlords like the Persians, Ptolemies, and Seleucids? Things changed with the death of Herod the Great, who was nominally a sovereign ruler even though he reported to Rome. His son Archelaus had the same arrangement but he displeased Rome, so henceforth Judea became officially a Roman province (or part of one, namely Syria). Jewish radicals led by Judas the Galilean rebelled: "Read my lips: no Roman taxes!" They believed paying Roman taxes amounted to, at best, collaboration with the enemy and, at worst, idolatry.

Jesus' critics are asking if Jesus agrees with the radicals. If he does, someone will surely rat him out! His response? "Render unto Caesar that which is Caesar's and unto God that which is God's" (Mark 12:17). This saying is popularly taken to endorse something like modern church-state separation or, worse yet, the sealing off of religion from mundane concerns, a perfect recipe for quarantining one's faith from one's everyday behavior.

But this interpretation is certainly mistaken. It overlooks the matter of *the coin*. Remember how Jesus asks for a volunteer from the audience to loan him a denarius, the Roman coin used to pay the tax. It is stamped with the profile of the emperor who reigned when the coin was minted. Roman coins could not be used to buy sacrificial animals in the Temple because of the scriptural prohibition of images. That's why there were money-changing tables in the Temple: if the only cash you had on you was Roman coins, which were fine for everyday commerce, you had to exchange them at the going rate. To buy your sacrificial animal, you needed Jewish or Phoenician coins which were not stamped with images. Problem averted!

So what's Jesus' point? There is no compromise in rendering (i.e., paying) Roman coins to Caesar since they belong to him in the first place and, in the second, you can't render them unto God in the Temple because he turns up his omnipotent nose at them and their idolatrous images. So there's no conflict, right? Indeed there is not. Does this place Jesus on the side of the Pharisees or anybody else? He is not talking about abstractions but about a specific case.

Finally, good luck with another saying, "Do not think I have come to bring peace. I have not come to bring peace, but a sword!" (Matt. 10:34).

ON THIS ROCK I WILL
ORGANIZE MY COMMUNITY

Was Jesus a community organizer? Some have thought so. John Howard Yoder, skirt-chasing Mennonite New Testament scholar,[1] floated an early version of this theory in his 1972 book *The Politics of Jesus*.[2] An Evangelical Christian, Yoder viewed Jesus in traditional theological terms plus the Anabaptist specialty of Jesus the pacifist. Yoder disliked the tendency of critics to deny certain sayings to the historical Jesus on the grounds that, as a proclaimer of the imminent Judgment Day, he could hardly have founded a church, an institution with rules of conduct and behavior such as we read in, say, the Sermon on the Mount and in Matthew chapters 18-19. Why bother, since there will soon be no ongoing world in which to govern one's mutual behavior? The problem is exactly like its Old Testament counterpart, the various Torah codes ascribed to Moses in the wilderness. They are anachronistic, predicated on Israelites already living a settled agricultural existence in Canaan. Clearly, these laws were formulated in Canaan/Israel, by Jews who lived there, to govern life and commerce there. Moses' name was borrowed to lend them clout. Ditto for the "church rules"[3] attributed to Jesus in the gospels.

Yoder, when not busy sexually harassing women at Goshen Biblical Seminary, came up with a way of circumventing the difficulty. He wanted *Jesus* to have said all those things, not some nameless Christian prophets or legislators. So here it is: what if Jesus viewed things

---

1   <peacetheology.net/john-h-yoder/john-howard-yoder's-sexual-miscon duct—part-one>

2   John Howard Yoder, *The Politics of Jesus* (Grand Rapids: Eerdmans, 1972).

3   Rudolf Bultmann, *The History of the Synoptic Tradition*. Trans. John Marsh (New York: Harper & Row, 1968), "Legal Sayings and Church Rules," pp. 130-150.

as Gandhi would two thousand years later: "Be the change you want to see"? Suppose he taught a kind of "realized eschatology," creating a proto-church already in this fallen, pre-messianic age? It would be a beach head of the soon-coming kingdom of God, initiating the sort of sanctified, harmonious lifestyle that would be universal in the coming kingdom, though swimming against the current until then. You know, the cost of discipleship[1] and all that.

Yoder was not really describing what Schweitzer had called an "interim ethic," because Schweitzer figured Jesus envisioned no social dimension. Rather, repentance was a matter of "every man for himself." (Remember the deck chairs on the Titanic?) Schweitzer had factored in what Yoder didn't, namely the utter discontinuity between This Age and the Age to Come. Who needs to be warned not to lust after his neighbor's wife (Matt 5:28) if the sons of the resurrection are like angels who neither marry nor are given in marriage (Luke 20:34-36)? Do you really need to be told not to hate or kill your neighbor (Matt. 5:21-22) when the redeemed will be one big happy family in the Millennium? Jewish Kabbalists[2] understood the point: the Torah could not survive into the kingdom of God without drastic transformation; otherwise, it must become a cobwebbed museum relic. Of all this Yoder seemed oblivious.

A newer version of "Jesus the community organizer" was popularized (at least within the scholarly fish tank) by Richard A. Horsley,[3] who just happened to be a community organizer himself. Coincidence? I don't have enough faith to believe that. John Dominic Cros-

---

1 Dietrich Bonhoeffer, *The Cost of Discipleship*. Trans. Irmgard Booth (New York: Macmillan, 1963).

2 Gershom Scholem, *On the Kabbalah and Its Symbolism*. Trans. Ralph Manheim (New York: Schocken Books, 1969), Chapter 2, "The Meaning of the Torah in Jewish Mysticism," pp. 32-86.

3 Richard A. Horsley, *Jesus and the Spiral of Violence: Popular Jewish Resistance in Roman Palestine* (Minneapolis: Fortress Press, 1993), Chapter 8, "The Renewal of Local Community, I: Egalitarian Social Relations," pp. 209-245; Chapter 9, "The Renewal of Local Community, II: Social-Economic Cooperation and Authority," pp. 246-284.

san[1] has made this Jesus model central to his (grossly anachronistic) reconstruction of the historical Jesus and Christian origins. We find it also in Elisabeth Schüssler Fiorenza's[2] discussion of Jesus' "discipleship of equals." Though these scholars are on the opposite end of the theological spectrum from Yoder, they share his interest in vindicating various dubious gospel sayings as actually the words of Jesus. "There's something about that name!" Namely its propaganda value.

Horsley, Crossan, and the rest picture Jesus as going village to village, organizing what Latin American Liberation theologians call "base communities,"[3] something like today's "sanctuary cities," a network of effectively autonomous shadow governments in which debt amnesty would be declared, patriarchal families and hierarchical authority would be dissolved, and Roman courts would be boycotted. One thinks inevitably of the People's Front of Judea in *Monty Python's The Life of Brian*.[4] It is all a lattice of transparently spurious Jesus quotes that Bultmann wouldn't have touched with a ten foot pole, which are then reinterpreted according to a modern Leftist agenda. Somebody apparently never read Henry J. Cadbury's classic book *The Peril of Modernizing Jesus*.[5]

Crossan envisions Jesus getting his sympathizers to give their mon-

---

1 John Dominic Crossan, *The Historical Jesus: The Life of a Mediterranean Jewish Peasant* (San Francisco: HarperSanFrancisco, 1991), Chapter 13, "Magic and Meal," pp. 303-353.

2 Elisabeth Schüssler Fiorenza, *In Memory of Her: A Feminist Theological Reconstruction of Christian Origins* (New York: Crossroad, 1984), Chapter 4, "The Jesus Movement as Renewal Movement Within Judaism," section 5, "Liberation from Patriarchal Structures and the Discipleship of Equals," pp. 140-154.

3 Ernesto Cardinal, *The Gospel in Solentename* (Maryknoll: Orbis Books, 1978).

4 Graham Chapman, John Cleese, Terry Gilliam, Eric Idle, Terry Jones, Michael Palin, *Monty Python's The Life of Brian (of Nazareth)* (New York: Ace Books, 1979).

5 Henry J. Cadbury, *The Peril of Modernizing Jesus* (New York: Macmillan, 1937).

ey to a common fund, as in the early chapters of the Book of Acts, and imperiously declaring the Levitical laws segregating lepers null and void, inviting them, stinking mummy bandages and all, to share the supposedly joyous table fellowship of "commensality." He and Horsley sound like they are describing the behaviors of a Melanesian Cargo Cult,[6] except that those modern apocalyptic social movements did all these things in order to trash the mores of this age, which is passing away (1 Cor. 7:29-31), and to exhaust their worldly resources, burning all bridges to the passing order. Those without the faith to do this must be shut out of salvation. In other words, they were by no means trying to set the ground rules for a new ongoing society to replace the old one. It was, again, an *interim* ethic.

But Albert Schweitzer was right on something else, too. In *The Quest of the Historical Jesus*, Schweitzer exposed the many previous historical Jesus reconstructions as mirror images of their authors' theological and social views. Jesus as a ventriloquist dummy. And Jesus the community organizer is the new Charlie McCarthy.

JESUS IN A PINK PUSSY HAT

Was Jesus a feminist? Some are pretty sure he was. Why? Some contend that Jesus is shown "breaking boundaries" that traditionally separated men and women in contemporary Jewish society. For instance, we are told that the story of the woman with the issue of blood shows Jesus tossing aside Levitical purity laws. Daring! Heroic! Feminist! Hold on there; read the story again. For one thing, Mark underlines the fact that Jesus *did not initiate the contact*; the woman did. For another, the feminist reading misunderstands the purity laws. The Torah by no means forbade a man to touch a woman while she was menstruating. It just stipulated that doing so would require a minor ritual purification. Ditto when it comes to touching someone with open wounds, or touching corpses. So did the Torah outlaw doctors or morticians? Absurd. Besides all this, do you really want to accept as data for

---

6 Peter Worsley, *The Trumpet Shall Sound: A Study of "Cargo" Cults in Melanesia* (New York: Schocken Books, 1968).

the opinions of the historical Jesus a healing story reminiscent of the extravagant testimonials at the Asclepius shrines? If we do, the whole endeavor is a charade—as I suspect it is.

In Luke 10:38-42 we see Jesus discoursing in a private home with friends. His hosts are women. One is busy with meal preparation, while the other sits at Jesus' feet, listening to the blessed words of the Savior. Aha! Rabbinical pupils sat in a circle at the teacher's feet! Does that mean that everyone who sits at another's feet listening to him is a rabbi in training? Close enough for feminist interpreters, apparently. But the mere idea of Jesus teaching a woman! That's pretty radical, right? At this point, advocates for a feminist Jesus love to produce a quote from Rabbi Eleazer (second century C.E.): "If any man gives his daughter a knowledge of the Torah, it is as though he taught her lechery." So once again, that radical rascal Jesus defies chauvinistic convention by teaching a woman! Or does he? Were religious Jews so misogynistic? Maybe not. If you look at the context, things look quite different.

> Ben Azzai says, "A man ought to give his daughter a knowledge of the Torah so that if she must drink [the bitter water, a test of chastity], she may know that the merit [that she acquired by Torah study] may hold her punishment in suspense." Rabbi Eliezer says: "If any man gives his daughter a knowledge of the Torah, it is as though he taught her lechery."

Now we see that Rabbi Eliezer's statement is to be understood as a rejoinder, rejecting the implicit use of Torah study as an indulgence enabling a well-educated adulteress to escape her due punishment. It is not fair to use this text, or half of it, to characterize ancient Judaism, making it look bad so Jesus will look good by contrast.

Was Jesus outraging decorum by daring to converse with the Samaritan woman (John 4:4-9, 27 ff.)? As Kathleen E. Corley[1] asks in a similar case, was Samaria like Wahabi-controlled Saudi Arabia? Were

---

1 Kathleen E. Corley, *Women & the Historical Jesus: Feminist Myths of Christian Origins* (Santa Rosa: Polebridge Press, 2002), is a devastating refutation of the feminist Jesus-ventriloquism I am rejecting here. Corley herself is a feminist, but she disdains any ideological hijacking of the text. (Her remark to which I refer comes from personal conversation.)

the codes *that* strict? The woman is indeed surprised that Jesus addresses her, but the issue is explicitly that of a Jew asking to drink water from a Samaritan's bucket.

The Achilles Heel of the feminist Jesus model is the utter lack of female names on the lists of the twelve. That is just deadly. Apologists for "biblical feminism" reply that for Jesus to have included, say, Mary Magdalene, Joanna, Salome, Susanna, and Mary and Martha of Bethany alongside Peter, Andrew, James, John, Matthew, and Judas, would have been just too controversial! Jesus had to accommodate his plans to the hardness of his contemporaries' hearts. This rationalization gives with one hand what it takes away with the other. The whole Jesus-feminist argument is that Jesus courageously broke with the all-pervasive male chauvinism of the ancient world. *Yay Jesus!* But suddenly we hear that, of course, he dared not ruffle feathers at *this* particular point! Which way *is* it? Obviously, this is just butt-covering exegesis.

All right then: forget the matter of "the twelve." Jesus *did* have female disciples, didn't he? I just listed six of them! But let's not read too much into that. The sketchy picture the gospels give us of these groupies following the itinerant guru and paying his bills (Luke 8:1-3) out of gratitude for his healing, teaching, and exorcizing them, recalls a pattern well known in the Hellenistic world—and long afterward. Nothing suggests Jesus' female devotees had any authority or positions of responsibility. A fan is one thing, a deputy quite another.[1]

---

1 Please bear in mind that I am not criticizing what I consider propagandistic versions of a political Jesus in order to default to one that I personally prefer. My own political opinions have nothing to do with Jesus, which is lucky for me, since I am afraid we must remain agnostic on the very existence of Jesus, much less what he may have thought about politics or anything else. But even if we were sure Jesus existed and that he taught either feminism or chauvinism, capitalism (as Bruce Barton, in *The Man Nobody Knows*, 1925, thought) or anarcho-syndicalism, pacifism or revolutionary violence, it would make no more difference to me than if we knew his favorite flavor of ice cream. (My friend Joseph Christopher remarked, concerning the topic of this paper, "I'm very interested in knowing what Achilles thought about nuclear proliferation." Bingo.)

IF THE BUGLE MAKES AN UNCERTAIN
SOUND, WHO WILL PREPARE FOR BATTLE?

So what? Since we cannot be certain of what political stance Jesus may have held, it must be sheer manipulation to choose one model and use it to command allegiance to the particular politics that one prefers. The only saying of Jesus I consider relevant to our topic is this one: "Why do you not decide for yourselves what is right?" (Luke 12:57). Don't take lazy short cuts. Consider the issues and to what extent your principles can be applied without adjustment to actual conditions. Where will you strike the balance between idealism and realism?[1] It takes work.

What's the alternative? If your approach is simply to obey Jesus in the gospels as if you were reading Chairman Mao's *Little Red Book*, you are begging the question of what he actually did teach. You will be making a false idol of whatever scholar who is using "Jesus" as a mouthpiece. You are allowing yourself to be manipulated. It's easier that way, after all.

But it is worse than that. Suppose you *could* be sure of Jesus' political views? And suppose you felt obligated to parrot them and obey them, come hell or high water? How would it not be theocratic fanaticism like that of radical Islam? They take Muhammad's word as law just as stubbornly as you take that of Jesus.

---

1 Reinhold Niebuhr, *An Interpretation of Christian Ethics* (New York: Living Age Books/Meridian Books, 1956), Chapter 4, "The Relevance of an Impossible Ethical Ideal," pp. 97-123.

Apocryphal Addenda:
More Lost Gospel Novels

In my 2010 book *Secret Scrolls: Revelations from the Lost Gospel Novels*[1] I examined over 40 (!) popular novels sharing the premise that someone had discovered a lost gospel or the bones of Jesus or both. The discovery becomes the focus of ecclesiastical attempts at suppression, international struggles to possess the relics for use in political blackmail, etc. The common assumption is that the making public of these relics would "blow the lid off" Christianity. My goal, besides indulging myself in reviewing the books *as* books, was twofold. First, I wanted to examine each book's depiction of New Testament scholarship and knowledge of early Christianity. Second, I sought to define precisely what each author supposed it would take to debunk the Christian faith. After all, the exhumation of the Nag Hammadi texts in 1945, though of great interest to scholars, hardly registered on the Richter Scale of popular religion. I would like, in the present article, to continue this analysis applied to several Lost Gospel novels which have appeared in the meantime or which somehow escaped my eagle eye before.

D.L. WILSON, *UNHOLY GRAIL*[2]

This fast-paced, character-driven novel belongs to the sub-subgenre of which Dan Brown's blockbuster *The Da Vinci Code*,[3] is perhaps the best known example, though Wilson's book is far superior. These books incorporate the conspiracy theory engineered by certain French

1 Robert M. Price, *Secret Scrolls: Revelations from the Lost Gospel Novels* (Eugene: Wipf & Stock, 2010).

2 D.L.Wilson, *Unholy Grail* (New York: Berkeley Publishing Group, 2007).

3 Dan Brown, *The Da Vinci Code* (New York: Doubleday, 2003).

neo-royalists who fabricated documents pretending to attest a long-lived Templar order called the Priory of Sion, which preserved the bloodline of Jesus Christ, the descendants of Jesus and Mary Magdalene, from which the Merovingian kings of France sprang. Of course, the cranks who launched this hoax claimed that *they* were entitled to the throne of France by virtue of their own imagined Jesus-Merovingian inheritance. The Jesus bloodline fantasy was popularized in the pseudo-scholarly 1983 book *Holy Blood, Holy Grail* by Henry Lincoln, Michael Baigent, and Richard Leigh.[1] In the wake of this publication, the bogus Priory of Sion lore was free for anyone's exploitation. To use it in one's novel in no way implies one is poaching from Dan Brown.

Joseph Romano is a hip, virile Jesuit priest who joined the priesthood on the rebound from a young romance spoiled by his interfering mother. She wanted him to marry someone closer to his station in life than the family servant girl he had chosen. But if not his beloved Marta, then nobody. Father Romano is a characteristically erudite Jesuit, a university professor of Church History. One day he receives an anonymous phone call from someone who promises to hand off to him the original autograph manuscript of a recently popularized Gospel of James. Father Romano, a noted expert in authenticating supposedly ancient texts, would love to get his hands on it, so he agrees to meet his mysterious informant in Grand Central Station. So he goes.

The anonymous caller is a no-show, or so it seems until a shot rings out, and in the melee that follows, someone rushes up to Father Romano and thrusts a box into his hands, then makes a hasty exit. But Romano puts this on the back burner while he makes his way to the shooting victim, an attractive young woman with a shoulder wound. She is Brittany Hamar. She was on the scene for the same reason as Romano, planning to meet an unknown caller offering to give her the Gospel of James papyrus. Britt, as she prefers to be called and is called throughout the novel, turns out to be a college professor of Christian

---

1 Henry Lincoln, Michael Baigent, and Richard Leigh, *Holy Blood, Holy Grail: The Secret History of Christ & the Shocking Legacy of the Grail* (London: Corgi, 1983).

Origins, which of course is why her caller chose her, he said, to receive the papyrus. But instead, it was a trap.

But Romano wound up not getting it either! Instead, the box contained the gun with which the shot was fired! The plot thickens. It gets even thicker when Father Romano visits Britt in the hospital. The two discuss their shared research interests, but their chat is not altogether friendly, for, while Romano is an orthodox Catholic, albeit genuinely as objective as he can be, Britt is an ex-Catholic embittered by the failure of God to answer her prayers. Her son died from Tay-Sachs disease, inherited from his father, Britt's husband, who blamed himself for his diseased genes—and killed himself! No help or comfort from the Man Upstairs. These events inclined the bereaved professor (who we may suppose is a fictionalized version of Elaine Pagels, similarly bereaved and likewise interested in Gnosticism[1]) to delve deeply into alternative ("heretical") varieties of early Christianity and their non-standard beliefs about Jesus. Her favorite is the belief in a bloodline descended from Jesus and Mary Magdalene.

Were such notions actually cherished by any early Christian sectarians known to us? Well, not quite, but sort of. The Valentinian Gospel of Philip famously says, "Jesus loved Mary Magdalene and often used to kiss her on the lips." This seems pretty clear, but in fact, in the larger context of Philip, the language, used more than once, of "kissing" and "conceiving" seems to be figurative, referring to the imparting of teaching and the realization of the (esoteric) truth. At any rate, it doesn't go so far as to say Jesus and the Magdalene were husband and wife. In 2012, Harvard professor Karen King promoted a papyrus fragment of something dubbed "the Gospel of Jesus' Wife," which (obviously) referred to Jesus' spouse. But this is why we need forensic specialists like Father Romano: it turned out to be a fake, playing on the current interest in the possibility that Jesus was married to the Magdalene. Protestant Reformer Martin Luther believed that Jesus married Mary Magdalene, but I know of no early Christian group who taught this.

---

1 Elaine Pagels, *The Gnostic Gospels* (New York: Random House, 1979).

But the notion of a "Jesus Dynasty"[1] is a viable, though admittedly speculative, theory, first set forth by Adolf Harnack and Ethelbert Stauffer.[2] A handful of early Christian references may plausibly be interpreted as implying a "Caliphate of James" analogous to the sequence of caretakers of the Islamic community after the passing of the Prophet Muhammad. James the Just, "the brother of the Lord" (Gal. 1:19) seems to have taken the reins of the Jerusalem Church after the death of Jesus, followed by the equally saintly Simeon bar Cleophas, another brother of Jesus. We hear also that the Emperor Domitian, fearing subversion, had a couple of innocent farmers brought in for interrogation in case they harbored delusions of messianic glory as descendants of the Jesus Dynasty. The trouble is, even if the "Caliphate of James" theory is correct, the dynastic succession moves laterally from Jesus to his brother James, then to a second brother, not through a son. James does, however, figure largely in *Unholy Grail,* as the new gospel ascribed to him seems to clinch the bloodline theory which Brittany Hamar plans to unveil to the consternation of the Catholic Church. Had the James Gospel disclosed the existence of his own role in the Jerusalem Caliphate, this would hardly be theologically dangerous. But the James text instead confirms that Mary Magdalene fled from Jerusalem to the South of France pregnant with Jesus' twins, a son and a daughter.

Aided by riches and relics unearthed beneath the site of Solomon's Temple by the Templars, who come in very handy in these novels, a secret group called *Deus Rex* ("God Kings") and *Le Serpent Rouge* ("Red Serpent," referring to the ongoing bloodline) safeguarded the descendants of Jesus, carefully arranging marriages to preserve the purity of the line. The cabal believed themselves to be stewards of the genetic legacy of Jesus, and thereby to provide the Second Coming of Christ when the time came.[3] An Inner Circle of five were themselves descen-

---

1 James Tabor, *The Jesus Dynasty: The Hidden History of Jesus, His Royal Family, and the Birth of Christianity* (New York: Simon & Schuster, 2007).

2 Ethelbert Stauffer, "The Caliphate of James." Trans. Darrell J. Doughty. *Journal of Higher Criticism* 4/2 (Fall 1997): pp. 120-143.

3 The same premise is crucial to the comic book and TV series, *Preacher.*

dants of Jesus, or believed so. Throughout the novel, four of them are murdered by a mysterious assassin calling himself Gabriel. (All five bore code names borrowed from the archangels Michael, Uriel, Raphael, Gabriel, and Melchizedek (often identified with Michael in Jewish lore). And of course this means that one of the Five had betrayed the rest, somehow coming to reject the whole bloodline business as heresy, preferring traditional Catholicism.

The involvement of Father Romano and Britt Hamar turns out not to have been accidental. Author Wilson deftly sets up this revelation with clues that at first do not seem to point in the direction at which they will finally arrive: Both protagonists are themselves descendants of the Messiah and the Magdalene! Unless, of course, the fanatical Gabriel, who reveals himself as Britt's hitherto-unsuspected brother (they were separated at birth), is right that the whole thing was no more than hoax and heresy. Gabe wires their secret headquarters to explode, with Romano and Britt locked inside together with the James manuscript and the mummified remains of Jesus Christ! But our heroes manage to escape, bearing away the papyrus with them. The place gets blown to Kingdom Come.

Romano demonstrates that the James Gospel is a forgery, but we do not learn who produced it. Come to think of it, neither can we be sure Gabriel was right. We are left to wonder if the protagonists as well as the Five pseudonymous angels really are/were descendants of Jesus and Mary Magdalene.

Suppose the James Gospel had been genuine and that Britt had published it, for that looked to be the danger Father Romano feared, to the discredit of his Church. Actually, the cat was pretty much out of the bag already. Remember, there had already been sensationalized coverage in the tabloids. Few take such hype seriously, and fewer still have the expertise to distinguish true reports of this kind from the fake ones.

Suppose Gabriel had not repented and gone trigger-happy? Suppose the appointed date for the Second Coming arrived and a Jesus descendant was waiting in the wings. Would the world be shaken? It would depend on whether Jesus, the progenitor of the Holy Bloodline, really had been the divine Christ or just a wise prophet. If the former, maybe the Millennium would arrive and the Five would be sitting pretty. If the latter, we would have a situation resembling that of Krishnamurti, a youth groomed by Theosophist leaders Annie Besant and Charles Leadbeater to be revealed as the next World Teacher, only, like Gabriel, he decided against it and flew the coop.

THE 13TH APOSTLE[1]

Our story begins with Professor Arnold Ludlow, who is deeply absorbed in reading a newly discovered diary written in the eleventh century by a monk, Brother Elias, located in the Weymouth Monastery in Merry Old England. The monk tells of his horror watching the burning at the stake of his best friend, a returned Crusader knight, William, who has been officially judged a heretic. This little weenie-roast is, of course, burning the heresy out of him so, once suitably fricasseed, he can go to heaven, which is not such a bad deal when you think about it, if the alternative is hopping around on Hell's griddles for eternity. But Elias didn't see it that way. But he dared not protest his friend's martyrdom lest he follow him into the flames.

What was the heresy that got William burnt at the stake? It wasn't exactly some eccentric belief he was peddling. Rather, it seems that he had brought back from the embattled Holy Land a remarkable scroll much resembling the famous Copper Scroll (or Cave 3 Scroll) from Qumran.[2] The latter has long baffled scholars of the Dead Sea Scrolls, unearthed in 1947 in the caves of Qumran. It purports to be a list of treasures rescued from the Jerusalem Temple just before the Roman siege began, in order to keep those rapacious Italians' mitts off them. The Copper Scroll gave the amounts and locations of treasure stashes

---

1 Richard and Rachael Heller, *The 13th Apostle* (New York: HarperCollins, 2007).

2 See John Marco Allegro, *The Treasure of the Copper Scroll* (Garden City: Doubleday Anchor Books, 1964). Joel C. Rosenberg's novel *The Copper Scroll* builds a story of espionage and eschatology around the Qumran Copper Scroll (the treasure list) and, like *The 13th Apostle*, posits a "new," related text, the Silver Scroll.

all over the countryside. But no one has ever been able to find them. So was the list a fake? A hoax? Some kind of improbable allegory about the quest for spiritual riches? Who knows?

That was not the scroll that William brought home. But his copper scroll was, if anything, a far greater treasure. For "the scroll William took from the cave contained the only firsthand account in existence of the life and the death of Jesus" (p. 84). It featured "Jesus' teachings, teachings dictated in His own words and recorded by one who lived at His side" (p. 207). Burnt at the stake for *that*? "Elias' diary bore testimony to a scroll that, during his time, was considered blasphemous. Apparently, it challenged the very foundations of Christianity" (p. 207). In other words, this scroll undercut and debunked the familiar canonical gospels, none of them authored by personal acquaintances or eyewitnesses of Jesus. The scroll gave the real story, and it was not the official one.

(By the way, for the orthodox bigwigs to want to suppress such a document need not have meant they didn't want to hear the truth, or to let anyone else hear it. If this had really happened, we can be sure they would have continued to believe the four gospels were genuinely apostolic and accurate, and that the "new" scroll was fabricated nonsense. After all, that's how the fourth-century bishops viewed the gospels ascribed to Thomas, Philip, Mary Magdalene, and others. These men were not scientific higher critics; they simply assumed that if texts didn't propound what they considered to be apostolic orthodoxy, they just *couldn't* be genuine.)

This novel does not actually deny apostolic authorship of the canonical gospels; it leaves that open. But if the gospel authors were really, as tradition holds, associates of Jesus, why does this "new" eyewitness gospel drastically contradict them? As the story proceeds, and we get to read the translated text, it develops that the twelve disciples were one and all Judases who were relieved to be rid of Jesus![1] His actual

---

1 See my *Deconstructing Jesus* (Amherst: Prometheus Books, 2000), Chapter 6, "Sacred Scapegoat," pp. 169-211. Seen through a Girardian lens, this idea is not so strange as it may sound. Years ago, when I presented that chapter to the Jesus Seminar (now in effect an arm of the Democratic Par-

teachings had caused enough trouble, put them in enough danger! So they set forth the familiar doctrines of the faith *instead* of what Jesus had taught.

As in all the many Lost Gospel novels, once the existence of the suppressed text becomes known, competing factions are urgent to gain possession of it, each for its own ends. Radical Muslims want it because they hope it will vindicate the Islamic Christology. "Once revealed, the secreted messages within these scrolls will prove beyond doubt that Jesus was nothing more than a mere mortal man and that the Church has been but a means to enslave its people as well our own" (p. 51). Actually, the speaker, a gent named Abdul Maluka, is referring to the Dead Sea Scrolls, but once he learns of the scroll of the thirteenth apostle, Micah ben Haggai, Maluka is convinced the newly discovered text will have the same utility.

But what *about* the Dead Sea Scrolls? The notion of the first-second century BCE Scrolls harboring shocking secrets inimical to Christian faith is as old as the discovery of the Scrolls, partly because of the mere possibility that they might, and, as time went on, partly because the elite cabal of Roman Catholic specialists in charge of the documents sat on a quarter of the Scrolls for decades,[1] refusing to let anyone else see them. Finally, in 1991, thanks to the efforts of Robert Eisenman[2] and others, the sequestered remainder of the Scrolls were revealed. Like the Scrolls already public for half a century, the new ones were quite fascinating, but there were none of the bombshells many had expected. Oh, there had been things to discomfit the faithful, but they were indirect. For instance, striking similarities between the organization of the Qumran monastery and that of the early church, as well as the apocalyptic terminology employed in both the Scrolls and the New Testa-

---

ty) some of the Associate members found the possibility intriguing, albeit distressing, so they approached John Dominic Crossan about it. Never fear, he assured them; go back to sleep.

1 Michael Baigent and Richard Leigh, *The Dead Sea Scrolls Deception*, (New York: Simon & Schuster, 1993).

2 Robert Eisenman and Michael Wise, *The Dead Sea Scrolls Uncovered* (Baltimore: Penguin USA, 1992).

ment, gave new support to the old theory of Renan that Christianity was essentially only "an Essenism."[1] And certain cryptic references to a "Teacher of Righteousness" who had been ambushed and killed at the hands of a "Wicked Priest" and whose followers anticipated his return at the End of Days, obviously implied a pre-Christian Jesus-analogue.[2]

The equivocal cipher language of the Scrolls makes it difficult if not finally impossible to reach definitive conclusions about the identity of the figures mentioned in the texts or even their socio-historical setting. Depending on how one was inclined to connect the dots, one might cast Jesus as the Teacher of Righteousness[3] or the Wicked Priest![4] Or one might understand the Teacher to have been John the Baptist or James the Just.[5] And so on. Any of these theories might disturb pious Christians *if true*, but they are all necessarily speculative and, as such, easy to dismiss (though I find myself persuaded pretty strongly by the interpretation of Eisenman). In view of this, it is clear that authors Heller and Heller are fudging the supposedly explosive "secrets the Dead Sea Scrolls held and that the Museum concealed from the public eye for decades" (p. 50). For instance, we read that

> The sum total of [Museum director Anton] De Vris' memos, speeches, and power votes helped squelch any actions—within and without the [Shrine of the Book] Museum—that might have allowed nearly all of the Dead Sea Scrolls to be put on public exhibition. The translations that would have followed would have most certainly challenged some of Christianity's most sacred writings. (p. 57)

---

1 Ernest Renan, *Histoire du Peuple d'Israel*, V, p. 70.

2 André Dupont-Sommer, *The Dead Sea Scrolls: A Preliminary Survey.* Trans. E. Margaret Rowley (Oxford: Basil Blackwell, 1952), pp. 98-100.

3 Cyril Glasse, *The Second Coming of the Judeo-Zoroastrian Jesus of the Dead Sea Scrolls* (Revelation: 2014).

4 Barbara Thiering, *Jesus the Man: A New Interpretation from the Dead Sea Scrolls* (Transworld Publishers, 1994).

5 Robert Eisenman, *James the Brother of Jesus: The Key to Unlocking the Secrets of Early Christianity and the Dead Sea Scrolls* (New York: Viking Penguin, 1998).

This is to perpetuate a long-exploded conspiracy theory, once reasonable, but no longer.

Abdul Maluka confides to his henchmen that, should the new scroll disappoint his hopes, instead confirming the traditional Christian belief, he will not hesitate to destroy it for the greater glory of Allah. As theologian Don Cupitt[1] once said, once things reach this point, we are no longer talking about *truth*, but merely about *policy*. And the same goes for an ultra-rightist group, the White Americans to Save Christianity, whose pious but ruthless CEO, Nathan McCollum, hopes "the scroll turns out to testify to the fact that Jesus was the son of God" (p. 119), but if it doesn't, he's got a match ready, too.

We do finally get to lift the veil and to see what all the shouting (and the killing!) is about. Chapters 37, 39, 43, 45, 47, 50, 52, 54 constitute the copper gospel of Micah, the thirteenth apostle. Before considering the substance, I want to comment on the style. Our novelists have no sense of what an ancient text would sound like, despite the fact that they actually have characters discuss what they think *was* ancient literary style. For instance, Sabbie (Sabra Karaim, by far the most interesting character in the book, a former Israeli commando, a multilingual translator, and a shrewd tactician) explains to her partner, Gil Pearson, that, even though the scroll narrates in the third person, it is nonetheless autobiographical.

> Two thousand years ago… no one would have thought to describe his own life in "I" terms. Everything was written as if it were a story about someone else. First-person wasn't even a known concept. Think about the Gospels from the New Testament. Imagine how odd it would sound if Luke said, "So, on this day, me and Jesus were discussing such-and-such, and this woman came up to us…." […] If you consider how little the individual mattered two thousand years ago, if you think about the fact that the "I" in storytelling didn't even exist… (p. 214)

But it's just not so. In fact, at the start of the very gospel to which Sabbie refers, Luke 1:3, the narrator refers to himself as "I." Acts, the se-

---

1 Don Cupitt, *The World to Come* (London: SCM Press, 1982), p. 143.

quel to Luke's gospel, contains several sections in the first person, the so-called "We narratives."[1] The (Apocryphal) Acts of John, written, like the canonical Book of Acts, sometime in the second century, has a section called "The Preaching of John," in which the elderly apostle recounts to his followers his recollections of the old days at the side of Jesus Christ. It is all in first-person. In fact, it sounds pretty much as Sabbie imagines Luke might sound in first-person narrative.

The closest thing to an ancient reticence to use the "I" in the New Testament would be Paul's account of his visionary journey to heaven in 2 Corinthians 12:1-10. In it Paul proposes to tell the tale of an unnamed "man in Christ" who received great revelations, then starts over, this time explicitly making himself the hero of the story. "A man in Christ" is revealed as Paul. But even here, the third-person narrative quickly gives way to the first person.

Even worse, the narrative of Micah's memoir is stylistically seamless with the other chapters of the novel. There were relatively long popular novels in the ancient world,[2] but they didn't sound like this. Heller and Heller make the same mistake Joseph Smith did in his Book of Mormon: both tell us that their fictive ancient narratives are being translated from thin metal sheets laboriously produced by pressing letters into the metal, but both the copper gospel and the Golden Plates are excessively verbose! No one with limited time and resources would ever permit themselves the inflated prolixity on display in both the Book of Mormon and the Micah memoir. At least Joseph Smith had a knack for simulating the style of an ancient book, something completely and ridiculously absent from the Micah scroll.

Who was the narrator?

In the section where they take Yeshua away, Micah tells us who he, himself, is... And the Gospels of Mark and John confirm it. The Gospels

---

1 Vernon K. Robbins, "By Land and by Sea: The We-Passages and Ancient Sea Voyages," in Charles H. Talbert, ed., *Perspectives on Luke-Acts*. Perspectives in Religious Studies Series No. 5 (Edinburgh: T&T Clark, 1978), pp. 215-242.

2 B.P. Reardon, ed., *Collected Ancient Greek Novels* (Berkeley: University of California Press, 1992).

describe a disciple who was there in Gethsemane, in the garden.... The disciple wore only a loincloth. This man was… "the disciple that Jesus loved." In the Gospels, John even talks about this disciple lying close to Jesus at the Last Supper, just as Micah describes his position at the Seder meal. (pp. 259-260)

First, the youth's garment, a *sindon*, is more like a night shirt, not a loin cloth a la Tarzan. Second, it is not "the Gospels," but rather only Mark who has the unnamed youngster just managing to escape a soldier's grasp by the skin of his teeth, leaving his flimsy garment behind. None of the other New Testament evangelists knew what to make of the odd incident and left it on the cutting room floor. If only the gospels came with a "Deleted Scenes" section! Third, "the disciple whom Jesus loved" appears only in John, who, remember, does not mention the linen-clad youth in the Garden of Gethsemane, so we have no right to say the New Testament identifies the youth as the Beloved Disciple. Heller and Heller's identification of the youth in the garden as the author of the Micah scroll is reminiscent of the theory, beloved of conservative apologists, that the youth was the evangelist Mark himself, making a cameo appearance in his own narrative, like Alfred Hitchcock popping up inconspicuously in his films, or Stan Lee in all the Marvel superhero movies. But that theory, a desperate attempt to make the evangelist Mark into an eyewitness of Jesus, is totally gratuitous.

We have seen that Christology was the chief object of curiosity among those eager for a glimpse of Micah's scroll. The Christian hoped it would attest that Jesus had claimed an identity as the Son of God, while the Muslim was betting the text would vindicate his faith's doctrine that Jesus was altogether human, not divine. But the scroll narrative as we read it never addresses this issue, at least not explicitly, though it seems to lean in the latter direction. What is Micah's understanding of Jesus?

Jesus explains the doctrine of the *tzaddikim* (righteous ones) to Micah (p. 253). Based upon the story of Sodom and Gomorrah in Genesis chapter 18, this Jewish doctrine[1] posits that in every era, the world

---

1 Solomon Schechter, *Some Aspects of Rabbinic Theology* (New York: Macmillan, 1910), p. 190. What a great book!

is preserved from destruction in retribution for its sins by the secret presence among the nations of a set number of righteous individuals (some traditions make it 50, others 36). These pious souls, humbly unaware of their crucial role, counterbalance the general wickedness of humanity. Though a tiny minority, the righteous are enough to count as the salt of the earth, preserving it from the wrath of a just God.[1]

In the version of Heller and Heller, there is in each millennium a single High Tzaddik whose special duties are three-fold. First, he must renounce/sacrifice his self-interest, the burden of guilt, all resentments and ambitions, much as Paul Tillich[2] said that Jesus had sacrificed all in him that was Jesus to that in him which was the Christ. And of course Jesus was the High Tzaddik of his age. Second, he must leave instructions of some kind to lead his next-millennium successor to Micah's scroll, which will describe his destiny and duty. Third, he must sing a sacred song of summoning (contained in the scroll), calling God to enter his soul and there, through his Tzaddik, to assess the worthiness of mankind, to discern whether there are sufficient *tzaddikim* to keep the world spinning.

If the High Tzaddik is prevented by death from completing his task, he may, in anticipation, appoint an immediate successor to complete his sacred work. Two thousand years ago Jesus was the High Tzaddik, and Micah, his Beloved Disciple, was his successor. Hence the creation of the copper scroll. We must infer that the crusader William was the Tzaddik of the previous millennium, with the monk Elias as his successor, who left the clues that guided the novel's protagonists to Micah's scroll. In the present day, a Syrian scholar, Sarkami, Sabbie's mentor, was the High Tzaddik. He, too, was finally murdered (by McCollum's thugs, frustrated in their pursuit of the scroll). Knowing what was to come, Sarkami passed the mantle on to Gil Pearson, a

---

1 My own Lost Gospel short story, "The Righteous Rise," in Vincent Sneed, ed., *The Dead Walk! Weird Tales of Zombies, Revenants, & the Living Dead* (Baltimore: Die Monster Die! Books, 2004) also involves the 50 Righteous, though in a very different way.

2 Paul Tillich, *Systematic Theology II: Existence and the Christ* (Chicago: University of Chicago Press, 1957), p. 123.

cyber-sleuth and expert in pattern-recognition, who had shared Sabbie's adventures throughout the novel.

Heller and Heller do not pretend the doctrine of the *tzaddikim* was first revealed in the sought-after scroll. The new secret was Jesus' role in that system of redemption. Was Jesus God's son? Was he a proto-Islamic prophet? Apparently neither: he was the High Tzaddik. Neither the Christian Christ nor the Islamic Apostle, he was the Jewish Righteous One. This "Christology" would ruffle the feathers of both Christian fundamentalists and Muslim zealots. But it is the Passion Narrative of the verbose Micah that would be poison to both. Heller and Heller posit a fate for Jesus more or less parallel to that ventured by Hugh J. Schonfield[1] in *The Passover Plot*. In Micah's account, Jesus had resigned himself to death on the cross, with no expectation of an Easter to follow, but his Beloved Disciple Micah, conspiring with Apollonius of Tyana and Joseph of Arimathea, contrives to give the crucified Jesus a mixture (like the Nindantera drug in the 1956 movie *The Black Sleep*) which will place him in a coma indistinguishable from death. Jesus is prematurely taken down from the cross and placed in a tomb. Micah is to bring the antidote to the Twelve to administer to the supine Jesus.

But, eavesdropping on them, Micah is shocked to hear the disciples deliberating whether bringing Jesus back would be a good idea at all. As already noted, they figure it would be best if they let Jesus die for real and for good. Micah gives them a false antidote, which he knows they will pour out, just to get them out of the picture while he uses the real one to restore Jesus. But the plan fails: the body of Jesus is beyond his reach. So Jesus dies and the Twelve fabricate stories of his atoning death, his glorious resurrection and ascension to heaven, his divine

---

1   Hugh J. Schonfield, *The Passover Plot* (New York: Bantam Books, 1967). Schonfield maintained that Jesus plotted his crucifixion to fulfill prophecies (as he understood them). He would survive by the application of a death-simulating drug, after which he should be nursed back to health by Essene allies. But the plan failed when the Roman soldier speared him in the ribs. Heller and Heller ascribe a similar plan to Micah, not to Jesus himself. But, as in *The Passover Plot*, the plan fizzles.

church, etc.[1] The holy hoax was off and running, and the truth had to trickle along as an underground stream.

There are several errors in *The 13th Apostle*, some of them pretty funny. The authors first call the Roman procurator "Pontius Pilot" (p. 209) but use the accurate spelling thereafter. They refer to a Roman "legionnaire," which should be "legionary" (p. 237). Legionnaires belonged to the French Foreign Legion.

Historical mistakes include the statement that Caesar Augustus' taxation census was carried out in Judea while Herod the Great was on the throne (p. 211), which was impossible since, under Herod, Judea was technically independent, albeit a satellite state, and this made it immune to the taxation to which Roman provinces were subject.

"Yeshua made his way to the Temple. When he discovered moneychangers plying their trade on this holiest of Holy Days, Yeshua was enraged beyond words" (p. 252). Too bad nobody told Jesus (and the Hellers) what everybody else knew: that the presence of moneychangers was necessary for the simple reason that pilgrims to the Jerusalem Temple from far away typically did not bring sacrificial lambs from their own herds back home because they had to be in good shape but might well break a leg on the trip. For the visitors' convenience, livestock was made available on site. And most people had only a purse full of Roman coins, which, bearing Caesar's portrait, were deemed "idolatrous" and thus could not be used for commerce in the holy precincts. Hence the moneychangers. Jesus couldn't have been surprised. His expulsion of these men can be plausibly explained in several other ways.

But the most egregious historical blunder occurs when Micah, who once studied as an Essene postulant at the Qumran monastery, recalls that "Flavius Josephus and I ventured there when we were under tu-

---

1 Hermann Samuel Reimarus similarly thought that, after Jesus' death, the disciples decided to cut their losses by reorganizing the revolutionary Jesus movement into a settled religious community, hoping to enrich themselves as its leaders. See Charles H. Talbert, ed., Ralph S. Fraser. *Reimarus: Fragments*. Lives of Jesus Series (Philadelphia: Fortress Press, 1970). I guess you could say it was a case of Max Weber's "routinization of charisma."

torage together [at Qumran]" (p. 297). Huh? Josephus the historian? You mean Josephus was a contemporary of Jesus Christ? Uh, Josephus was born in 37 CE, some seven or eight years after the crucifixion! And besides, Josephus only took the name "Flavius" after the Jewish War in 73 CE, when he switched teams and kissed the butt of the Flavian Emperor Vespasian. (And did I catch the use of the first person in that passage?)

You may think I am making too darn much of these goofs. It's just a drugstore paperback, for Pete's sake, right? But are gross historical mistakes more excusable in historical fiction than in straight history writing? I suppose that historians' errors are more serious, but novelists' goofs are equally misinformation. Personally, I think the use of mistakes in fiction is a cheat, like the use of obscenities in humor. If you really had any creative imagination you wouldn't have to resort to cheap shortcuts.

But *The 13th Apostle* is a novel, and it is a lively, creative, and exceedingly well crafted one.

THE FIRE GOSPEL[1]

Michael Faber's book is a bit different from the other Lost Gospel novels I discuss here, and that in two ways. For one, the narrative tone is subtly comedic, even sort of flippant. It has a definite, and quite effective, satirical edge to it. And this approach works very well, perhaps all the more because the premise of a shocking gospel discovery has been worked over so many times (not to imply the others do not manage to have their own originality; they do). Second, more than most of the other books, this one places a magnifying glass on the huge repercussions of the discovery on the life of the discoverer, then opens the view to the wider impact on the world at large. Finally the two plot lines converge, as the discoverer finds he cannot take refuge in a safe bubble of individual privacy.

One of the most fascinating features of the Lost Gospel novels is the scenario in which the controversial document is uncovered. In *The*

---

1 Michael Faber, *The Fire Gospel* (New York: Grove Press, 2008).

Fire Gospel it is pretty straightforward, a bolt from the blue. Theo Griepenkerl, a linguistics professor at a Toronto university, is on a business trip to a ruined antiquities museum in Mosul, Iraq. His job is to negotiate the five-year loan of what relics remain after the wartime looters have left. If the Iraqi authorities agree to the loan, the Canadian university will see that the Iraqi museum gets rebuilt and refurbished. These discussions are rudely pre-empted by the explosion of a series of bombs in the street right outside the museum. The curator is vaporized, but Theo manages to escape largely intact by hurrying down the stairwell to the basement. As he passes a huge wall sculpture of a very pregnant woman, her expectant belly cracks open like an egg, spilling nine exceptionally well preserved papyrus scrolls. Theo manages to get them out of the country without incident, seeing in them an opportunity for fame and fortune, all the more once he gets a good look at them back home in his Toronto suburb.

Together they constitute a long epistle in the form of answers to questions sent the author by several members of an unnamed first-century Christian community. (First Corinthians has basically the same format.) And who is the author? You know him. He is Malchus, the servant of the high priest whose ear Simon Peter clipped off in the Garden of Gethsemane, in the melee coincident with Jesus' arrest. Naturally interested in the outcome of these events, the bandaged Malchus tags along with the arresting party leading Jesus back to the palace of High Priest Caiaphas, Malchus' master. He witnesses the crucifixion and burial of Jesus, and what he sees and hears converts him to faith in the slain Messiah. Though the disciples Thaddaeus and James later claimed to have been on hand, Malchus has no memory of their presence. No other of the twelve darkened the foot of the cross, though subsequently, perhaps under the influence of drugs, the disciples had visions of Jesus as he was before Calvary. In these visions they received various new teachings from Jesus (much as in the Gnostic gospels).

Malchus' diary reveals him as a self-pitying hypochondriac who seems to talk more about his sad sack self than about Jesus. What he writes cannot properly be called a gospel, at least not in the usual sense of the term, since he tells only of the few events (albeit major ones) he himself observed. He was never in a position to hear any of Jesus' teachings for himself, though of course he learned them from the disciples with whom he was henceforth associated. He says how even Jesus' closest students differed in their interpretations of what he said.

The importance of Malchus' account lies in the fact that it is an Aramaic document earlier than the canonical gospels, and that its authorship claim is not in doubt, combined with the more sober, prosaic, and uncomfortable reportage it preserves. And this despite the overtly adulatory prose in which these details are placed. Here is *the* ideal case for the famous "criterion of embarrassment": there is no way a Jesus-admirer would ever have made *this* stuff up. Jesus panics as the Romans prepare to nail his hands to the cross. Once crucified, his bowels evacuate and he urinates, spattering Malchus' upraised forehead—some anointing! In the Garden Jesus did not restore Malchus' severed ear (contradicting Luke, though not Matthew, Mark, and John). His last words from the cross were "Please, somebody, please finish me!" (Well, "My God, my God, why did you forsake me?" isn't that much better, I guess.) All this was too much for Simon (Zelotes, I think, but possibly Peter), who repudiated his faith and became "a whore-mongering drunkard." No Joseph of Arimathea in sight.

As daunting as some of this stuff sounds, the text that author Faber "re"-produces for us does not come across as an anti-Christian burlesque. And the fictive evangelist Malchus does seem to grasp the (Pauline) paradox of the "scandal of the cross," that the divine Son condescended to share the lowest depths of degradation that mankind is heir to. Far from debunking Jesus as the Messiah, these revolting events might be the best demonstration of the meaning of the Incarnation. "Was it not necessary for the Christ to suffer these things and only then enter into his glory?" (Luke 24:26).

Still, once Theo goes to press with his translation and commentary (a process reminiscent of the PR hubbub over the possibly spurious "Gospel of Judas" in 2006), he learns that his best seller *The Fifth Gospel* does debunk and shatter the faith of some readers, even driving some to suicide. Others die in a book-burning that gets out of control. Eventually he realizes that, deep down, that his goal all along had been to discredit Christian faith, in order to free people from its shackles.

One disgruntled reader pulls a gun on him, though he is rescued. But finally he is abducted by a pair of fanatics who accidentally burn down the bookstore where he was promoting the book. These blazes prompt a witness to quip that the book ought to have been titled *The Fire Gospel*. Who are his abductors? One is a Muslim who fears that, if Christianity is destroyed, most of the disappointed Christians will convert to Judaism, strengthening Israel's position against the Palestinians. The other is a kind of Docetist who believes Jesus was a hologram projected by the united attentions of those who believed in him. (It is not quite clear what he would have found objectionable in a text that has Jesus say, "Of what am I composed? I am composed of all who believe in me." But the guy is pretty confused.)

Anyway, this pair of crazies force Theo to record a false confession that he faked the whole thing, made it all up. After this, one wants to kill him, the other to let him go. The latter prevails after clubbing the former, and Theo, wounded and dizzy, staggers in the general direction of a hospital. He makes it there only by the kindness of strangers. We are left to reflect on the fact that Theo himself has undergone sufferings not dissimilar to those of Malchus' Jesus. We may infer that the experience demonstrates the redemptive truth that Jesus' sufferings were those of Everyman. And we are left to wonder if Theo is even going to bother trying to set the record straight: will he take the trouble to repudiate his televised confession? Does it matter anymore?

THE BLOOD GOSPEL

This massive novel[1] posits the existence of a revelatory text written by Jesus Christ, using his own blood for ink. We never to get to read much of the text, except to learn that an apocalyptic war will be impending in the generation in which this Blood Gospel is discovered, and that the book will be opened by "a Woman of Learning, a Warrior of Man, and a Knight of Christ." Of course, these three will turn out to be the three protagonists of the novel, predictably beautiful archaeologist

---

1 James Rollins and Rebecca Cantrell, *The Blood Gospel* (New York: Harper, 2013).

Dr. Erin Granger, predictably brawny Sergeant Jordan Stone, and not surprisingly pensive Father Rhun Korza. The book relates the complex and action-packed tale of their desperate quest to locate the lost volume before the bad guys can. These last are called "the Belial," as if that were a collective term. In effect, it serves as an abbreviation of the "Sons of Belial," the nefarious "Sons of Darkness" mentioned in the Dead Sea Scrolls. "Belial" (also "Beliar") means "Man of the Lie" and denotes the Antichrist. See 2 Corinthians 6:15a, "What accord has Christ with Belial?" Here the Belial are a conspiratorial league of vampires and their evil human abettors. Their leader is a shadowy figure referred to (till the very end) simply as "He" or "Him."

Indeed, vampires are absolutely central to this fascinating novel. Authors James Rollins and Rebecca Cantrell ask us to imagine a secret arm of the Catholic Church composed of repentant, clerically ordained vampires, the Order of the Sanguines, whose mission has been to fight the unrepentant blood-suckers. Father Korza belongs to the Order. You see, becoming a vampire destroys one's soul, but one may win redemption by joining the Sanguinists. Once sworn in, a vampire assuages his blood-thirst only by partaking of the sacramental blood of Christ, transubstantiated wine! I call this a brilliant stroke of the inventive imagination! And you can see why the novel swallows Roman Catholicism hook, line, and sinker. This would never work on Protestant assumptions!

In *The Antichrist* Nietzsche commented thusly: "The Christian and the anarchist are both decadents… they are both incapable of acting in any other way than disintegratingly, poisonously and witheringly, like *blood-suckers*. Christianity was the vampire of the *Imperium Romanum*." In *The Blood Gospel* this is literally true. The Sanguines (a pun on the lay order of the Beguines?) were founded by Jesus when he called his friend Lazarus from the tomb (John Chapter 11). It seems Lazarus was not dead but rather *un*dead. He had somehow fallen victim to a vampire, and his relatives, unwilling to stake him, just sealed him into a tomb before he could avail himself of anyone else's hemoglobin. But Jesus set him loose, telling him redemption was still possible on the terms already mentioned. Lazarus became the undying head of the Order.

What Rollins and Cantrell are doing here is an exotic species of Rationalist exegesis. The old Protestant Rationalists of the eighteenth century posited non-supernatural explanations for biblical miracles. Trying to retain belief in the factual accuracy of the Bible, they had sacrificed any notion of divine interventions to their new belief in Newtonianism, which envisioned the world as a great self-regulating machine requiring no "mid-course corrections" by the Designer. Thus Jesus was feeding the peckish multitudes with fish and bread handed to him from a secret Essene kitchen in a cave behind him! He didn't rise from the dead but only swooned on the cross and woke up in the tomb, then rejoined his disciples, etc. The twentieth century witnessed a revival of Rationalist exegesis with a scientifictional twist: the gospel miracles were all wrought by means of advanced science by Jesus, himself the result of flying saucer aliens inseminating Mary with space-sperm. Thus his healings were like those of Dr. McCoy, roaming the halls of a 1980s San Francisco hospital, in *Star Trek IV: The Voyage Home*.[1] What we have in *The Blood Gospel* is such a re-reading, only it is (fictional) vampirism being read in between the lines rather than Newtonianism or Extraterrestrialism. And, for my money, it works great![2]

One of the things I like so much about these novels (as well as their cousins, the Antichrist novels[3]) is the display of what we might call *profane theological speculation*. The authors are free to let their theological imaginations run in channels neither established nor sanctioned by any doctrinal orthodoxy. This book is a perfect example of such free myth-making.

The vampiric Order of the Sanguines exists in its own parallel world of underground chapels, vestments, rituals, and theology, something analogous to the Catholic missionary strategy of "indigenization," the

---

1 See Robert M. Price, *Night of the Living Savior* (Amherst: Prometheus Books, 2013).

2 Another example from the novel is the Herodian Slaughter of the Bethlehem Innocents, which turns out to have been a vampire feeding frenzy.

3 See Robert M. Price, *The Paperback Apocalypse: How the Christian Church Was Left Behind* (Amherst: Prometheus Books, 2007).

translation of various features of Roman Catholicism into forms more familiar to, and compatible with, non-Western cultures. But in one sense, Sanguinist Catholicism is not entirely fictive. It embodies the religious (Catholic and High Church Anglican) devotion of the Decadents at the close of the nineteenth century, explored and documented so well by Ellis Hanson in his book *Decadence and Catholicism*.[1] What was it about Roman Catholicism that so fascinated people like J.K. Huysmans and Oscar Wilde? To them Catholicism seemed to be in terminal decline (the ecclesiastical equivalent, perhaps, of the creaky Austro-Hungarian Empire) and thus redolent of the burning glories of the setting sun and autumn foliage. The Romanticism of the Decadents saw Catholicism as a last stand against soulless Modernity. They reveled in the rich aesthetics of Catholic vestments, architecture, incense, and ceremony. They resonated with the melancholy of repentant shame, seeing in it the very medium of grace. And we might better understand the rife occurrence of priestly pederasty today by comparison with the homoeroticism of the Catholic Decadents.

Decadent Catholicism is fundamental to the conception of the fictive Order of the Sanguines, focusing on Father Korza. He is constantly tormented by self-reproach over an event from centuries before when he gave in to his love and lust for a beautiful and aristocratic countess. In embracing her, he sank his fangs into her tender throat. It was a climax of erotic ecstasy for them both. But was it worth the burden of guilt that came with it? One feels that these bouts of plaguing self-reproach are themselves a kind of ecstasy for the fallen priest. Here is the rich but cursed transgressive love so important to the Decadents, lacking only the homoerotic element. Father Korza has much more depth of character than either Jordan or Erin, important as they are to the story. One might say, a la Henry James, that in Father Korza's case events are illustrations of character, while with the other two character is the sum of events.

No novel is completely unique, and it is interesting (to me, at least) to note several significant parallels between *The Blood Gospel* and the

---

1 Ellis Hanson, *Decadence and Catholicism* (Cambridge: Harvard University Press, 1997).

trilogy *The Strain, The Fall,* and *The Night Eternal* by Chuck Dixon and Guillermo del Toro.[1] These books just preceded *The Blood Gospel* in appearance. It is conceivable that they influenced *The Blood Gospel,* but who knows? And so what? It wouldn't be plagiarism. Anyway, both stories call the vampires by the Hungarian term *strigoi,* a good choice given how cliché the word "vampire" has become. Both have a shadowy master villain pulling the strings in a scheme to dominate and corrupt the world. Both turn out to be still-living biblical characters (though the TV version of *The Strain* never gets around to telling you that The Master was one of the angels sent to report on Sodom and Gomorrah. He kind of liked what he saw and remained on earth as a vampire!). Both feature a herd of vampirized youngsters serving the villains. Both count among their heroes a reformed, teetotaler vampire. In *The Strain* he's Mr. Quinlan, born a hybrid human/vampire (like the protagonist of the *Blade* movies and Marvel comics they're based on)[2] back in ancient Rome. Father Korza is even closer to a superhero in Kurt Busiek's comic book *Astro City,*[3] He is The Confessor, a Batman analogue who is a vigilante Catholic priest and secretly a fanged vampire..

Perhaps the most interesting element is the crucial role of an ancient, one-of-a-kind book needed to avert planet-wide catastrophe. In *The Strain* the book is the *Occido Lumen.* Great pains are taken to acquire and to protect the book, but viewers of the TV adaptation were left wondering why it all came to nothing, the result of late-in-the-day veering off the plot of the novel and its sequel. I suspect intrusive editorial bungling with an original script.

I have noted the absence from *The Blood Gospel* of any attempt at biblical criticism, but I could not help taking note of three brief

---

1 Guillermo del Toro and Chuck Hogan, *The Strain* (New York: William Morrow, 2011); Del Toro and Hogan, *The Fall* (New York: William Morrow, 2012); Del Toro and Hogan, *The Night Eternal* (New York: William Morrow, 2013).

2 This may be no coincidence, since Guillermo del Toro lurks behind both the *Blade* films and *The Strain.*

3 Kurt Busiek, Brent Eric Anderson, and Will Blyberg, *Astro City: Confession* June 23, 1999.

passages, admittedly taken out of context, which are nonetheless relevant to the higher critic.

> "You are skeptical of religion, but steeped in biblical knowledge. As a result, you see things that nonreligious scholars could miss. Likewise, you question things that religious scholars might not. It was that rare combination that made you perfectly suited to bring the Gospel back to the world." (p. 254)

> "Over the centuries, many famous historians had died, taking their undocumented knowledge with them to the grave." (p. 314)

> "I exist in a state halfway between damnation and holiness." (p. 289)

The sequel to *The Blood Gospel* is *Innocent Blood*[1] (a reference to Judas' "seller's remorse" in Matt. 27:4: "I have sinned in betraying innocent blood"). The Blood Gospel figures into this one as well. We are not, however, granted any more clues as to the "scene of writing" of a text written by Jesus using his own blood as ink. When are we to imagine him penning it? Luke 22:44 has Jesus agonizing so severely in the Garden of Gethsemane that he sweats blood. Did he whip out a legal pad and start writing until the goon squad got there to arrest him? But we do get a bit more text to play with. The first book gave us this much:

> A great War of the Heavens looms. For the forces of goodness to prevail, a weapon must be forged of this Gospel written in my own blood. The trio of prophecy must bring the book to the First Angel for his blessing. Only thus may they secure salvation for the world.

In this second novel we get a bit more. After various wild adventures, our heroes have qualified to see more of the text. Recalling the gradual opening of the seven-sealed scroll in Revelation chapters 6-8, the disclosure of more text of the Blood Gospel is gradual, each new glimpse presupposing events occurring since the previous glimpse was grant-

---

1 James Rollins and Rebecca Cantrell, *Innocent Blood* (New York: Harper, 2014).

ed. In fact, the ancient pages are at first blank until the right moment for the right person (the Woman of Learning, Dr. Granger) to read them, like the next clue in a scavenger hunt.

> The Woman of Learning is now bound to the book and none may part it from her.
>
> The Warrior of Man is likewise bound to the angels to whom he owes his mortal life.
>
> But the Knight of Christ must make a choice. By his spoken word, he may undo his greatest sin and return what was thought forever lost.
>
> Together, the trio must face their final quest. The shackles of Lucifer have been loosened, and his Chalice remains lost. It will take the light of all three to forge the Chalice anew and banish him again to his eternal darkness.

This last bit is a "coming attractions" preview of the third novel in the series.

Of this text a couple of things may be said. First, the whole thing sounds more like Nostradamus than the Jesus of the gospels. And why all the cipher language? Does Jesus want to get this job done or not? Well, of course it is all equivocal in order to provide riddles for the protagonists to solve and to keep the narrative unfolding. Second, it sounds like Jesus is writing this text *now*, sending up to the minute updates to his earthly agents. I think of Isaac Asimov's *Foundation* trilogy, where, at crucial points in the story's progress, the holographic image of "psycho-historian" (futurologist) Hari Seldon pops up to interpret the current situation, which he had anticipated centuries before (when these holo-image messages were recorded) and advises what to do next.

There is another secret gospel in this book, not a written text but rather a sequential bas relief molded or carven into a huge buried disk of volcanic glass. It depicts the story of Jesus' very first miracle. He was an adolescent and kind of screwed it up! He threw a rock at a white dove during the Holy Family's sojourn in Egypt. He meant only to startle the bird but wound up killing it. So, in order to undo his error, young Jesus resurrected the dove. This miracle registered on Lucifer's radar, and he promptly showed up to attack our boy. Just as quickly, the Archangel

Michael intervened to defend Jesus from Lucifer, his old foe during the rebellion of the fallen angels (repeated, or depicted in a flashback, in Revelation 12:7-9). Not content to remain on the sidelines, Jesus ignited a spiritual solar flare. Lucifer slunk away from ground zero wounded and bleeding, but Mike got the worst of it. He was ripped asunder into three fragments, which, in the course of these novels, were implanted in various mortals, most recently three of the characters in these books, accounting for their extraordinary powers. One of these bearers of Michael's angelic essence is, not surprisingly, Sergeant Stone. The second is an adolescent lad named Tommy Bolar, a cancer victim miraculously healed by the angelic infusion. The third is Judas Iscariot.

What, you may ask, is *he* doing here? One of the fascinating features of the novels in this "Order of the Sanguines" series is the presence of historical characters long thought dead but who still abide on earth. Rasputin is one (surviving as an undead vampire). Countess Elisabeth Bathory is another. And, from biblical days, Lazarus of Bethany and Judas the Betrayer. What Rollins and Cantrell have done is to combine the gospel character Judas with the legendary figure of the Wandering Jew (variously called Ahasuerus, Cartaphilus, and Battadeus), the jerk who heckled and punched Jesus on his way to Golgotha.[1] Jesus, not in a particularly forgiving mood, understandable given the circumstances, cursed this detractor to wander the earth for all the centuries till the Second Coming. Obviously, both Judas and the Wanderer are symbolic of the Jewish people as Christians viewed them: cursed by God for their refusal to believe in Jesus, sentenced to pass the ages in exile from their homeland. Implicitly the two characters are equivalent, almost the same villain at two successive points in the Passion Narrative.

So Judas is not a vampire. His prolonged existence is the result of Jesus' command. But Rasputin is a good choice for a vampire since history tells us he was shot, stabbed, poisoned, and drowned—and still survived, though not for long. He sounds like horror villains Michael Meyers and Jason Voorhees. And as for Countess Bathory, she is a nat-

---

1 Joseph Gaer, in *The Legend of the Wandering Jew* (New York: New American Library/Signet Books, 1961), pp. 76-77, ascribes to ancient Gnostics this same identification of Judas Iscariot with the Wandering Jew.

ural choice for a vampire since she was likely part of Bran Stoker's inspiration for Count Dracula, Vlad the Impaler being another. The historical Bathory was a radical Calvinist who believed that, God's election being unconditional, no act of a believing Christian could count as a sin. A very vain woman (not unlike the Queen in *Cinderella*), she consulted the spirit resident in her mirror on how to preserve her beauty and was instructed to bathe in the blood of virgins. And at last count, she killed some 900 of them in her cosmetological quest.

I see a rather big problem with Rollins's and Cantrell's capping-off of the Judas subplot. Remember the nefarious and despicable (Sons of) Belial from the first book, *The Blood Gospel*? The absolutely fiendish leader of this bunch turned out to be none other than Judas. His black-hearted villainy continues unabated into *Innocent Blood*, where we learn his murderous schemes are all part of an attempt to release Lucifer from his confinement in Hell so he can ravage the earth and its wretched inhabitants. And why would Judas want to do this? To end his centuries of marking time until the Second Coming of Christ. So he's trying to commit "suicide by cop," prompting the apocalyptic return of Jesus. (The same strategy was employed by the angel Gabriel in the 2005 movie *Constantine*, who wanted to get things moving.)

But it doesn't seem Judas has been having all that bad a time for two millennia! He has become a vastly wealthy corporate magnate and a connoisseur of the finer things. Not to mention his on-and-off affair with Arella, a defrocked but still noble angel who protected the infant Jesus and moonlighted as the Cumaean Sybil. Once Judas finally does die, from a thrust from Michael's rediscovered sword (which short-circuits his immortality), his soul ascends, hand-in-hand with Arella to heaven! Isn't that getting off pretty light for a guy whose betrayal of Jesus Christ was actually the *least* of his countless crimes? It is a victory not of righteousness, but only of romance novel sentimentality.

The saga concludes in *Blood Infernal*,[1] most of which requires no comment here given the particular scope of our concern with these books. But we do at long last learn the true nature of the long lost Blood Gospel.

---

1 James Rollins and Rebecca Cantrell, *Blood Infernal* (New York: William Morrow, 2015).

When the bulk of the pages, hitherto blank, finally disclose their text, it becomes evident that the whole thing was written to Lucifer! You see, back in Eden (which turns out to have been located in Nepal!), Eve had welched on a deal with the Serpent (i.e., Lucifer). Though the devil informed her that the Tree of Knowledge was good for food and desirable to make one wise, he was apparently incapable of grasping the fruit himself and was dependent upon someone with an opposable thumb to get him some. The agreement was that Eve and the devil would share the knowledge contained in the fruit. But that hussy Eve for some reason kept the fruit and the knowledge for herself. (The whole business does not make sense and is never clarified.) But for want of this knowledge Lucifer became (or continued as?) the villain known to history.

What crucial information did Eve gain that Lucifer did not? We never really find out, but to Lucifer (who appears in person toward the end of this third book) it is saving knowledge. Jesus has told him he can yet be redeemed (somehow or other) and returned to heaven. But that can hardly be the knowledge Eve received, since, once she bit into the fruit, it was downhill all the way! And why had God waited all those millennia to appoint the "trio of prophecy" to deliver this knowledge to Old Scratch? Beats me.

At least one can say that the *Blood Gospel* trilogy defies the standard formula. The possibility of its publication to a shocked world never really comes up. And, though it supplements the standard biblical epic, it certainly does not threaten conventional Christian faith, as these "new" gospels always seem to do in the vast majority of Lost Gospel books. Quite the contrary: the whole novel absolutely depends on the literal truth of all the stories of the Bible: Adam and Eve, the miracles of Jesus, the whole nine yards.

THE TESTAMENT[1]

Call me pedantic, but this novel makes two mistakes that, though small, betray a surprising ignorance of the subject matter. Author

---

1 Eric van Lustbader, *The Testament* (New York: Forge Books/Tom Doherty Associates, 2006; rpt. London: Head of Zeus Ltd., 2015).

Eric van Lustbader uses "prophesies" as a noun. The noun form is "prophecies." "Prophesies," on the other hand, is a verb. The product of someone prophesying is a prophecy. People who don't know that (including editors and proofreaders) probably think "prophesies" is a noun because they also use the neologism "prophesize" as the verb form where they should use "prophesy." Or else they first heard other ignorant folks use "prophesize" and forgot the difference between "prophesy" and "prophecy." Chicken or egg? Similarly, Van Lustbader constantly has characters refer to the Book of Revelation as "Revelations."[1]

None of this reflects on Eric van Lustbader as a fiction author. *The Testament* reveals him on every page as an expert wordsmith and plotter. The book exceeds 500 pages, and they are absolutely packed with locomotive-paced action, a superb thriller. The book offers a breathless sequence of headlong action, clever plot twists, and ever more shocking revelations. Such novels have these traits in common with action movies as well as superhero comics. But *The Testament* does not come across as one of these. Why? Van Lustbader imbeds the *story*, which by itself might seem wildly contrived, lacking all plausibility, in a rich setting of world-building *discourse*.[2] Scenes replace one another in rapid-fire succession, and every time they do, the author paints vivid pictures of each exotic location, including relevant historical background and very creative metaphorical descriptions of nature, architecture, and local color, plus striking character description. The seamless interpolation of interior monologue and narrative mind-reading is both profound and sharply perceptive. Things change so radically and so quickly, one fears becoming

---

1 How ironic that carping mockers of Donald Trump ridiculed him for referring to "Two Corinthians" instead of "Second Corinthians," thinking the candidate was ignorant when in fact he was using, whether he knew it or not, the now-common scholarly idiom.

2 See Gérard Genette, *Narrative Discourse: An Essay in Method*. Trans. Jane E. Lewin (Ithaca: Cornell University Press, 1980); Seymour Chatman, *Story and Discourse: Narrative Structure in Fiction and Film* (Ithaca: Cornell University Press, 1978).

confused but never does. At least that was my experience reading the book.

As Van Lustbader explains in an "Author's Note" at the end of the long tale, he has based his story's premise on real, though far less spectacular, historical fact, namely the fourteenth-century dispute between two factions of the Franciscan Order. The Conventuals were sheltered monastics yet did not accept Saint Francis' rule of voluntary poverty (though, as cloistered monks, how could they *not*? I don't get it). But their rivals, the Observatines, did. Also, they did not hide their light under the bushel of a secluded monastery but instead became wandering mendicants, seeking to spread Francis's gospel far and wide. In 1322 Pope John XXII ruled in favor of the Conventuals (and their allies the Dominicans), condemning the requirement of voluntary poverty. Van Lustbader (or the historians he read?) suggests that the issue was not really religious, but a matter of *realpolitik*, an attempt to suppress Observatine attempts to spread their power and influence far beyond Rome. And they did in fact make their way Eastward, where much of the novel takes place.

Van Lustbader makes this group a Gnostic sect (as if anybody would actually name their group "the Gnostic Observatine Order" any more than Magneto would have dubbed his organization "the Brotherhood of Evil Mutants"). Once ensconced in the Middle East, the brethren managed to dig up esoteric treasures, especially including a document (or a fragment of one; it doesn't seem consistent), the *Testament of Jesus Christ*, Jesus' own account, apparently, of his ministry. In it he discloses his secret use of "the Quintessence" to heal the sick and to raise the dead, notably Lazarus of Bethany. This magical substance was the Fifth Element sought by medieval alchemists. Somehow Jesus found it, which sounds like a pretty fascinating story, here untold, all by itself! It is described as a kind of oil amenable to evaporation if the vial is not tightly sealed.

Other secrets cherished by the Gnostic Observatines are less sublime, more secular, for it seems that, in order to support their behind-the-scenes work of mercy, relief, and peace-making, these ascetical activists are not above utilizing bribery and blackmail, preferring the methods of the Borgias to those of Francis of Assisi. For instance, their nuns don't mind serving as holy hookers in order to coax juicy information from politically powerful bedmates.[1]

The Observatines find their opposite number in the Knights of St. Clement of the Holy Land, a wildly fictionalized version of the historical Knights of St. John of Jerusalem from Crusader days. Van Lustbader imagines them as the (semi-autonomous) Black Ops arm of the Vatican, ready to commit any bloody atrocity for the sake of the Roman Catholic Church. They are aware of the valuable secrets long held by the Observatines and have for centuries striven to usurp this information to advance their own agenda. Just now, they are desperate to secure for themselves the Quintessence with which they hope to rejuvenate the failing Pope, lingering at death's door. Though their goals have long since been largely secular under a mere veneer of religious devotion, they do prize this Pope's support and do not relish the prospect of finding themselves orphaned under a new Pope who may not back them.

I must pass over the meat of the book and concentrate on the elements that place *The Testament* in the Lost Gospel genre. How important to the novel is the eponymous *Testament of Jesus Christ*? It seems to me, not very. The focus is on the Quintessence, and it almost seems as if Van Lustbader intends this autobiographical gospel merely as an instruction sheet for using the alchemical healing balm. Why is the Quintessence to be kept secret? Because, its guardians reason, if widely known it would introduce a flood of less than altruistic consequences, e.g., ensuring the age-long reigns of tyrants who might obtain it, consolidating the power of undying elites over their ephemeral subjects. Fair enough, I guess. But is the accompanying *Testament* controversial in its own right? Yes, but for reasons that defy my analysis. As in John LeCarre's Lost Gospel novel, *The Gemini Contenders*, the conception of the dangerous text is incoherent and grossly self-contradictory. Van Lustbader has obviously derived the fictive vol-

---

1 Cf., the Flirty Fishy Ministry: Miriam Williams, *My Fifteen Years as a Sacred Prostitute in the Children of God Cult* (New York: William Morris, 1998). The theme of hooker espionage is not new. See, for example, N. Leo Lancer, "They Saved Rockwell's Brain" in *Risque Stories #5* (March 1987).

ume from Morton Smith's discovered (or fabricated) Secret Gospel of Mark.[1] He knows we possess only a fragment of Secret Mark, preserved in an ostensible letter from Clement of Alexandria. To match this, he sometimes speaks of the Observatine *Testament* as being only a fragment (though other times he implies the whole thing is extant). I am surprised he did not say the Observatines possessed a complete copy of Secret Mark in order to smuggle the Quintessence business into it. That would have been simpler.

But what disclosures in either Secret Mark or the *Testament of Jesus Christ* would have been so disturbing to the Vatican? Here we encounter total confusion.

> Basically, the Secret Gospel [of Mark] has been derided by Bible scholars because it depicts Jesus as a miracle worker, which runs counter to formal Church doctrine. It describes in detail how Jesus resurrected not only Lazarus, as is told in the eleventh chapter of Clement, but this boy and others as well. (p. 211)

Let me get this straight. Jesus being a miracle worker, a healer, runs afoul of orthodox Christian doctrine? Has Van Lustbader ever bothered to read the New Testament gospels? As anyone else knows, they are full of stories in which Jesus heals the sick and raises the dead. Far from being rejected by the Church, these miracles have for centuries been the staple of Christian apologetics. And what is this about an account of the raising of Lazarus in the eleventh chapter of *Clement*? What the hell?! Van Lustbader is thinking of the Gospel of John, chap-

---

1 Morton Smith, *The Secret Gospel: The Discovery and Interpretation of the Secret Gospel According to Mark* (New York: Harper & Row, 1973); Smith, *Clement of Alexandria and a Secret Gospel of Mark* (Cambridge: Harvard University Press, 1973); Stephen C. Carlson, *The Gospel Hoax: Morton Smith's Invention of Secret Mark* (Waco: Baylor University Press, 2005); Peter Jeffery, *The Secret Gospel of Mark Unveiled: Imagined Rituals of Sex, Death, and Madness in a Biblical Forgery* (New Haven: Yale University Press, 2007); Robert M. Price, "Second Thoughts on the Secret Gospel" *Bulletin of Biblical Research* 14/1 (Spring 2004), pp. 127-132.

ter eleven. He gets "Clement," I guess, from the letter of Clement of Alexandria, which contains the (supposed) fragment of Secret Mark. (Did anybody proofread this thing?)

True, many scholars are on record denouncing the Secret Gospel of Mark, but hardly because *like all the others*, it depicts a miracle-working Jesus. Rather, it is because they believe the whole thing was Morton Smith's little joke. In Van Lustbader's Author's Note he revisits this notion of scholarly reluctance to accept Secret Mark.

> Not surprisingly, its authenticity is disputed by many biblical scholars, who do not believe that the historical Jesus was a miracle worker. However, that is precisely how the Secret Gospel of Mark portrays him. (pp. 551-552).

Again, our author is hopelessly confused. He seems to imagine that most biblical scholars share the dogmatic biases of Roman Catholicism, which he imagines forbid us to think Jesus worked miracles. He is vaguely aware that biblical historians reject the gospel miracle stories as unhistorical, and that most of them dismiss Secret Mark as a modern forgery, but he has no idea how these facts fit together. As far as Secret Mark is concerned, in question is not what the historical Jesus may or may not have done, but rather whether Secret Mark is really an ancient Christian writing like the Gospel According to Thomas, or rather a twentieth-century hoax.

But that's not the end of it.

> If it was the Quintessence that resurrected Lazarus and not Jesus' divine power, then the stories of him being a healer, the stories that the Church has systematically repressed, are true. And it might also be true that when he died his disciples resurrected him using the Quintessence. (p. 212)

Huh? Again, this absurd notion that the Catholic Church suppressed the stories of Jesus as a healer! They sure didn't do a very good job of it! They're all there in every Catholic edition of the Bible. Stupid enough, but it gets even worse. The *Testament of Jesus Christ* would vindicate those stories, and this would be bad because "The entire structure of the Catholic faith would crumble because it would call into question whether Jesus was, in fact, the son of God" (p. 212). The nearest I can come to making sense of this gibberish is that, while the gospels *do* have Jesus healing by his innate divine powers as God's son, the *Testament* gospel would reveal that he was merely doing what anybody else could do provided he had a supply of the Quintessence on hand. But all this presupposes that the Church agrees that Jesus *was* the healer the gospels, including Secret Mark, make him. The bone of contention would be the source and means of those miracles. Hoo boy! Get your story straight!

Finally, Van Lustbader tells us that Secret Mark was suppressed in the fourth century. There is no such information. Where does he get this date? I am guessing he is referring implicitly to the Council of Nicea in 325 C.E., where, according to groundless popular imagination, the bishops selected the books that would henceforth constitute the official New Testament, rejecting numerous others, such as the Gospels of Thomas, Philip, Peter, etc. Such decisions were not made at that Council. Nor do we have reason to believe the Nicene bishops had even heard of the Secret Gospel of Mark (if it existed at all before Morton Smith!).

THE CHRISTOS MOSAIC[1]

This exciting page-turner rivals Van Lustbader for vivid place and scenery descriptions and sharp insights into its characters. The prose waxes poetic and sparkles, yet it transitions smoothly into fierce action scenes with ingenious weapons exchanges and choreographed violence. You are there! One of the genre conventions of thrillers is the rapid succession of reversals in which allies turn out to be enemies and enemies secret friends. The risk here is arbitrariness, and *The Christos Mosaic* does feature a couple of instances of what one might call "*devil ex machina*," but post facto explanations seem to justify them even though we (I) couldn't see them coming.

But our business here is to measure the novel's treatment (and ex-

---

1 Vincent Czyz, *The Christos Mosaic* (Saint Louis: Blank Slate Press, 2015).

ploitation) of New Testament scholarship. As ever, no criticism attaches to a novel's fictive speculations and imaginary events, e.g., archaeological discoveries. But we are obliged to point out errors of fact which are quite a different matter. And in a book of over 500 pages there are bound to be some. As James Orr said of the Bible itself, to gripe about a few errors of detail here and there in scripture is like faulting a beautiful marble statue because one can detect a few grains of sand in the surface texture. The same is true of this novel. Let's review a few of these, just to be pedantic.

"Saint" Origen, as author Vincent Czyz dubs him, was not a canonized saint of the Catholic Church. He was instead retroactively condemned as a heretic for views considered unorthodox in light of subsequent theological developments. Similarly, "Saint" Hegesippus was not considered a saint for the simple reason that, as our author himself informs us, he was a Jewish-Christian Ebionite, thus automatically deemed a heretic by the Catholic Church. Other fact-goofs include a reference to "First Galatians," as if there were a Second, and the claim that the evangelist Matthew could not read Hebrew, which he plainly did since he used not only the Greek Septuagint but also both Hebrew and Syriac versions of the Bible when each fit his purpose.

Author Czyz thinks Herod the Great meant to extinguish the Hasmonean (Maccabean) dynasty when he had its last male heir drowned in a swimming pool, but in fact Herod attempted to claim Hasmonean legitimacy by marrying Mariamne, the granddaughter of Hyrcanus II, a Hasmonean king. He confuses the virginal conception of Jesus (with no human father) with the Immaculate Conception of Mary (from two parents but without the usual transmission of Original Sin). He says "Simon" was a Hebrew name, when in fact it is Greek, though plenty of Jews named Simeon (Shimon), which *is* a Hebrew name, called themselves "Simon" when doing business with Greek-speakers. He refers to the "Clementine Institutes" when he means either the Clementine *Recognitions* or the related Clementine *Homilies*.

But let no one imagine that Vincent Czyz has not done his homework. His representation of contemporary New Testament theory and scholarly speculation is spot-on. He is significantly influenced by the work of Burton L. Mack, Robert Eisenman, Early Doherty,

Frank R. Zindler, and myself.[1] From that some readers will be able to anticipate the nature of the "shocking truth" that so threatens Christianity that some are ready and willing to kill to prevent its disclosure.

It seems that two important ancient scrolls have been ticking away like long-fused time bombs ready at last to explode. One is a more complete copy of the Habakkuk Commentary, one of the most important Dead Sea Scrolls. New text in it enables a dating in the first century C.E. It speaks, albeit vaguely, of the murder of the Teacher of Righteousness, leader of the Dead Sea sect. A few early scholars posited that the Teacher, never named, was none other than Jesus, but others discounted the possibility because they preferred a first- or second-century B.C.E. date. The later date established by this (fictional) new manuscript does *not* support the identification of Jesus and the Teacher. No, the disturbing implication is that the Teacher, not said to have been crucified or resurrected, *cannot* have been Jesus. But the first-century C.E. date does press the question of why a document like this makes no mention of Jesus any more than Josephus or Philo did.

The second manuscript is a copy of the Q Document in the original Aramaic. It vindicates Burton Mack's stratification of Q into Q1, Q2, and Q3. Mack notes that the earliest stratum, the original version of Q before its scribal augmentation, had nothing to say of Jesus' ministry, miracles, crucifixion, or resurrection. It was essentially a collection of sayings reflecting the radical wisdom of the Cynics Diogenes and Antisthenes. Mack infers from this that the historical Jesus was an itinerant sage like Diogenes, no messiah, no son of God, no divine incarnation. Mack expected this conclusion to rock, if not to sink, the Christian boat. But Czyz goes an important step farther, adopting the theory shared by Earl Doherty and myself that the ascription of these sayings to Jesus (or to any one sage) was secondary. Originally Q1

---

1   For a critique of my and Doherty's view about Q, see Christopher B. Zeichmann, "Fear and Loathing in a Lost Gospel: A Response to Some Radical Uses of the Sayings Gospel Q with a Focus on Its Formative Stratum." *Journal of Higher Criticism* 12/2 (2006), pp. 37-49.

must have been an anonymous digest of Cynic teachings. Christians liked them and attached Jesus' name to them.

Then who *was* Jesus? There *was* no historical Jesus. He was an amalgam of James the Just (identified, a la Eisenman, as the Teacher of Righteousness), John the Baptist, Simon bar Giora, Judas of Galilee, and others. This would explain why it is notoriously difficult for scholars to harmonize and homogenize the gospel sayings, which point in very different directions. The problem is solved if the gospel sayings stemmed from several very different historical, prophetic, and messianic figures.

Paul complicated matters further when he transformed the Jesus figure into a Hellenistic dying-and-rising savior deity. He had started with Philo's belief in a heavenly Man, the Logos, God's agent in creation. This version of Jesus Christ, Paul thought, had never set foot on planet earth but was slain by evil archons in the heavenly spheres above the earth. In time, Mark had brought Jesus down to this sublunar realm, drawing upon rewritten Old Testament sayings and stories, as well as early Christian sayings still surviving here and there in the epistles without ascription to Jesus.

The book's title, *The Christos Mosaic*, refers to this composite character of the gospel hero, the fictional Jesus Christ. The attentive reader (whether of the novel or of my account here) will notice that the Mythicist conclusion at which protagonist Drew Korchula arrives does not stem from the (fictive) discovery of Q1 but is drawn from the speculative work of radical New Testament scholars like myself. The importance of the imagined discovery is really no more than to corroborate the hypothetical stratification of Q. By itself, it would by no means prove the non-existence of a historical Jesus.

In our analysis (here and in my *Secret Scrolls*) we have asked what our authors thought it would take to "blow the lid off" Christianity. The discovery of Q1 would not by itself do that, but in this novel the unearthed Q1 functions as shorthand for Mythicism. And when it comes to light, there is controversy, to be sure, but there turn out to be few ramifications. Scholars, predictably, dispute the significance of the find and especially the Mythicist inferences drawn from it. The Christian public is generally unfazed. If they even hear of it, it must sound to them like an idle debate in the irrelevant ivory towers of egg-head academia. And no doubt that is exactly what would happen.

But in the story, the existence of the Q1 Document does galvanize two rather specialized groups. Just as in Van Lustbader's *Testament*, we witness the struggle between two ancient religious factions. Answering to Van Lustbader's Knights of Saint Clement of the Holy Land are Czyz's Sicarii, historically the assassins belonging to the revolutionary Zealot party in first-century Judaism. These modern Sicarii are not in direct continuity with their ancient counterparts but are an offshoot of the Knights of Malta, an order which does indeed exist today. The fictionalized version of these Knights will go to any lengths to suppress the disclosure of Q, not wanting to take the risk of it discrediting the Catholic Church. Corresponding to the Gnostic Observatine Order in *The Testament* are the Ebionites in *The Christos Mosaic*. The historical Ebionites were early Jewish Christians who deemed Jesus a righteous mortal whose perfect character won God's approval to such an extent that he rewarded him with a heavenly throne at his right hand. These Ebionites seem to have petered out in the fourth century C.E., but Czyz's Ebionites are imagined as a clandestine continuation of that group. Czyz writes them as long being privy to the truth now rediscovered by Drew, which is why they are determined to safeguard the Q scroll and to have it published. It will, they think, vindicate their ancient, secret belief that James the Just was the true Messiah and that Jesus did not exist.

Surprisingly, it develops that the Roman Catholic Sicarii are defending a belief they themselves do not hold! They are like Dostoyevsky's Grand Inquisitor, perfectly willing to feed the faithful masses the pabulum of fairy tales, lest these fragile souls awaken to a truth which will terrify them (and make them harder to control). They know there was no Jesus, but they want to do their flock the dubious favor of hiding the troubling truth from them.

The great irony of this book is that both factions think the Q manuscript is powerful/dangerous enough to kill and to die for, whether to reveal it or to destroy it, whereas, once revealed, it has almost no impact!

STIGMATA[1]

This 1999 movie must be discussed here even though there is no book version. In it Gabriel Byrne plays Jesuit priest Andrew Kiernan, a travelling investigator of what we might call Catholic X-Files: reports of weeping or bleeding statues, spontaneous healings, Marian apparitions—and lost gospels, of which the film tells us some thirty-five have come to light, though never shared with the public for fear that such inconvenient revelations might rock, or even sink, the ecclesiastical boat. My guess is that this motif was inspired by the shameful history of the Roman Catholic custodianship of the Dead Sea Scrolls, unavailable to anyone outside the elite team of (not coincidentally) Roman Catholic scholars into whose hands they were early on entrusted. Father Kiernan is dispatched to check out the anomalous case of an atheist stigmatic. She is a hairdresser (even though she herself is in desperate need of one!), one Frankie, portrayed by Patricia Arquette. She is convincingly written and acted as someone simultaneously naïve yet jaded, and with no patience for faith.

Eventually the stigmata she bears prove to be but the prelude to a much worse sequence of floggings by no visible lash, thorny gashes about the forehead, and the Damoclean prospect of an unseen spear thrust which must prove terminal. While comatose, she gets busy filling a wall of her apartment with Aramaic script, a language she does not know. It soon develops that Frankie had recently been given, simply as a curio, an antique rosary that, unbeknownst to her, had been the property of a recently deceased priest, Father Alameida.[2] This old scholar had been translating a newly unearthed gospel text that was deemed too hot to handle. He realized the Church would suppress or destroy it, so he absconded with the manuscript, taking refuge in remote Brazil, where he continued laboring over it until death interrupted him. Frankie's acquisition of the old man's rosary (stolen off

---

1 Written by Tom Lazarus and Rick Ramage.

2 Portrayed by Jack Donner, who appeared as Romulan Subcommander Tal in a 1966 episode of *Star Trek*, which, combined with his role in *Stigmata*, ought to make him a *Romulan Catholic*, right?

his corpse by some kid at his funeral) allowed the spirit of Father Ala-meida to possess her. He was, of course, the original stigmatic whose intense piety had made him a target for Satanic torments. Now poor Frankie is his unwilling proxy, which of course explains how an atheist hairdresser can be manifesting the holy wounds of Christ.

Frankie's wall full of Aramaic was the text of the fugitive gospel. We are told it was the actual pre-church record of Jesus' own words. And what was so objectionable, so dangerous, about *that*? In other words, in terms of our inquiry, what was it in this gospel that would threaten to blow the lid off traditional Christianity? Well, you see, the text has Jesus say, "The kingdom of God is inside you and all around you, not in houses made of wood and stone." Uh, we wouldn't want that bit of information to get out, would we? People might take it seriously and stop attending church altogether, and the vast cathedrals might decay into crumbling ruins like the extinct castles that dot the British coun-tryside. And lots of ecclesiastic bureaucrats would find themselves on the Eucharistic bread line.

Needless to say, the Church fat cats do find out about this and try to prevent publication. Cardinal Daniel Houseman (Jonathan Pryce) plays Grand Inquisitor, trying to strangle Frankie even as he prays for her. Just as in Dostoyevsky's parable, the Catholic Church feels obliged to silence any echoes of the voice of the radical Jesus in order to relieve the flock of the terrible burden of freedom and free thought that Jesus would have cruelly imposed upon them. But, no surprise, Father Kiernan rescues her, and the lost gospel's voice will be heard.

The passage quoted above is readily recognizable as a slightly fudged version of saying 3 from the Gospel of Thomas. In fact, fol-lowing the movie is a postscript that pretty much admits that the film is a fictionalization of that gospel, seeking to bring its message to a wider audience.

Again, we have to ask if the lost gospel's revelation would cause so much as a blip on the public radar. Apparently not, since Thomas has been available in numerous translations for decades now (I my-self have preached from it many times), and the churches still thrive. There is, to be sure, a growing legion of young people who consider themselves "spiritual but not religious," and this anti-institutional turn has wounded the established churches, from Roman Catholics to Evangelical Protestants. But there are many factors involved, among which the Gospel of Thomas is but a very minor note. Interest in it by non-scholars is the result of this movement, not the cause of it.

Besides, didn't we already have this anti-institutional gospel message available in texts like Luke 17:20-21 ("The kingdom of God is not coming with signs to be observed, nor will men say, 'Here it is!' or 'Over there!' For the kingdom of God is within you.") and John 4:21, 23-24 ("The hour is coming when you will worship the Father neither on this mountain nor in Jerusalem… The hour is coming, and now is here, when the true worshipers will worship the Father in spirit and truth, for the Father seeks such people to worship him. For God is Spirit, and those who worship him must worship in spirit and truth."). Yes, of course we have it, but has it been taken seriously? The goal of *Stigmata* is try to make it heard again.

One thing seems to escape us when we wonder why most Christians are complacent pew potatoes. For one thing, these radical-seeming texts are embedded in larger documents which foster and reinforce passive obedience to church tradition and institutional authority. Passages such as Luke 17:20-21 and John 4:21-14, and their implications, are thus rendered anomalous notes of dissent, hard to hear over the booming tones of Matthew 16:1-19 and of the Pastoral Epistles. They represent a still, small voice, and only a scant few have ears to hear it. It has always been so. Keep in mind that Thomas is a Gnostic gospel, part of the Nag Hammadi collection. And this cache of writings was hidden away to shield them from destruction at the hands of the ecclesiastical book burners. Gnostics did not organize themselves into churches, preferring to exist on the margins of Catholic parishes, meeting in clandestine study groups.[1] That is how one pursues a communal form of religion based on anti-institutional scripture.

---

1 Peter Brown, *The Body and Society: Men, Women, and Sexual Renunciation in Early Christianity.* Lectures on the History of Religions. New Series, Number 13 (New York: Columbia University Press, 1988), p. 118.

Did Paul Think of the Pre-Incarnate Christ as God?

How did Paul regard the pre-existent Christ? Was he already deity, or did deity, as humanity, come only later for this being? Paul had no hesitation about predicating of the exalted Christ what he would normally say of God,[1] but what of Christ before the exaltation? In order to attempt to answer this question, this paper will examine Pauline texts which treat the subject of the pre-human state of Christ, as well as those which seem to call Christ "God." The working hypothesis will be that Paul's pre-incarnation Christology is based on the contemporary concept of hypostatized Wisdom/Primordial Adam, the begotten/created agent of creation. Godhood, on the other hand, was a category reserved by Paul for the exalted Christ.

The earliest document likely to have contributed to a concept of personified Wisdom is the Book of Proverbs. There Wisdom is a creature of God and is in turn either the agent of the rest of creation or at least attendant at the scene (Prov. 8:22-31). Wisdom arrives among men, trying to save them from folly and turn them from the error of their ways (8:1-4ff). This personification is primarily a literary device in Proverbs, but it seems to be taken more and more seriously as a hypostatized divine attribute/mediator of God in later literature. In the Alexandrian work, The Wisdom of Solomon, more is said of Wisdom. She sits beside the divine throne (9:4). She assisted in creation (8:6; 9:2, 9). She is "a pure emanation of the glory of the Almighty… a reflection of eternal light, a spotless mirror of the working of God, and an image of his goodness" (7:25-26). She was born at a particular point in time (8:3), and her "coming to be" is placed at the "be-

---

1 Walter Elwell, "The Deity of Christ in the Writings of Paul." In Gerald F. Hawthorne (ed.), *Current Issues in Biblical and Patristic Interpretation* (Grand Rapids: Eerdmans, 195), pp. 297-308.

ginning of creation" (6:22). Wisdom is in possession of the riches of God's knowledge (8:4-5). In the book of Wisdom of Jesus ben Sirach, Wisdom is clearly described as having been created prior to the rest of creation (1:4, 9; 24:8-9). Her role as agent of creation is not so clear, but something similar seems to be implied (1:9-10; 24:3). She is sent to earth to enlighten men (24:6-12, 19-23).

Similarly, in 1 Corinthians, Paul describes Christ as God's Wisdom having come among men (1:21-25). He was also the agent of creation (8:5-6). The letter to Corinth is particularly concerned with opposing the worldly, elitist gnosis or wisdom of Corinthian pneumatics, by explicating the true wisdom of God, i.e., Christ (crucified). In another context, where not only wisdom but also the nature and role of Christ are at stake, Paul develops the Christ-Wisdom idea still further. The Colossian church had adopted (or adapted) a system of cosmological speculation, wherein Christ was placed in the context of a pantheon of angelic Powers as merely one more mediator between the Pleroma of God and the world. This *Sitz-im-Leben* makes the ensuing discussion particularly valuable for the present consideration, since Paul will be concerned to define specifically the proper Christology. According to his schema, Christ himself holds the Pleroma of the Godhead (1:19; 2:9-10). His is the treasure of wisdom and knowledge (2:3; cf., Wis. 8:4-5). Like (or *as*) Wisdom, Christ was the agent of creation (even of the creation of the angelic Powers) (1:16). Accordingly, he was born before the rest of creation (1:15) in the pattern now familiar from earlier Wisdom speculation. The title "first-born of all creation" seems to imply more than a status metaphorically comparable to that of a first-born son, i.e., being named preeminent heir for whatever reason, not necessarily biological descent. This is strongly indicated by the parallel clearly drawn between 1:15 and 1:18: Christ is the first-born of the dead—he has preeminence over the rest of those to be raised from the dead since he was the first one (chronologically) to be raised. Likewise, he is the first-born of creation—he has preeminence over the rest of created things since he was the first one (chronologically) to be created. (Of course, he was in turn instrumental in creating everything else (e.g., 1 Cor. 8:6), just as he will be instrumental in raising everyone else.)

The Christ-Wisdom is called, in the Colossians passage, the "image (εικων) of the invisible God" (1:15), just as Wisdom is called "an image (εικων) of his goodness" (Wis. 7:26). This characterization is taken up again in the Pauline literature in such a way as to suggest the presence of another important Christological image. In 2 Corinthians 4:4 Paul writes that Christ "is the image (εικων) of God." Similarly, the "face of Christ" reveals the "glory of God" (4:6). In 1 Corinthians 11:7 it becomes clear that both "image" and "glory" are terms denoting man as being "created in the image of God" (Gen. 1:27). These hints that Christ is a special Adam-figure are confirmed by explicit argumentation in 1 Corinthians 15:45-49. In Romans 5:14ff Christ was contrasted with Adam in an explanation of how universal salvation as well as universal sin could come about, each through a single individual. In 1 Corinthians 15, however, Christ is actually described as a new Adam, to explain the role of the resurrection of believers in the plan of redemptive history. First he shows how humanity had to bear the body of mortal, fragile flesh, or "dust" (15:49). This was patterned after the first Adam, the "man of earth" (v. 47). But humanity is destined for better things, the immortal, superhuman glory of the resurrection body, on the pattern of the second Adam (v. 49), the "man of heaven." Christ was constituted as the new Adam by his resurrection. This was his creation as "life-giving Spirit" just as Adam's formation from clay was his creation as a "living soul" (v. 45). Thus the resurrected Christ as the new image of God, just as Adam was created in God's image.

But the Colossians passage described the pre-incarnate Christ as already being the image of God. This should offer a hint that the heavenly Adam idea is not solely an exaltation motif for Paul. The Christological hymn of Philippians 2:6-11 does in fact develop the concept further in the direction of the pre-incarnate Christ already being the heavenly Adam, the "form," εικων (= image) of God. The purpose of introducing this hymn is to exhort the quarreling Philippians not to strive for their own interests (2:1-5). The thought is the equivalent to Jesus' warning that one should not exalt himself above his fellows lest he be humbled. Rather, one should humble himself below his rightful status and will then be exalted (Luke 14:11). The hymn reinforces this advice with the example of Christ himself. It recounts how the Primordial Adam, bearing the form (image) of God, as did his counterpart the historical Adam, did not yield to the temptation to go and seize actual equality with God as did the historical Adam (Gen. 3:5; cf., Isa. 14:12-15). Thus he was not humbled to subjection to death as was his counterpart. Instead, he actually humbled himself "unto death" voluntarily. He was then elevated to the formerly unsought prize of equality with God. Upon him was bestowed the divine Name with all its prerogatives.[1]

Thus, for Paul, the pre-human Christ could be described as both the Wisdom of God and the Primordial Adam. The term "image of God" is common to both, but is this mere coincidence? On the contrary, it points to a single concept in contemporary religious thought: that of the Wisdom/Word of God being both the Primal Man and the agent of creation. Some of the relevant surviving literature is old enough to indicate possible influence on Paul, while other works are at least part of the same milieu and seem to stem from the same kind of speculation. Thus some significant conceptual parallels might be expected. The thinker closest to Paul in time and worldview is John. In his gospel, John clearly links the Word of God (a figure with numerous Wisdom associations) with the pre-existent Son of Man from Above. In 1 Enoch, the Son of Man (= "the Man") is a heavenly Man named before creation, in a manner reminiscent of Wisdom. Even so, John speaks of the Son of Man who came down from heaven (John 3:13). The relevance of John's pre-incarnational Christology will be picked up later in the present study.

Philo is another near-contemporary of Paul who seems to have moved in a related world of ideas. For him, too, these two concepts are related. The Logos is the image of God, as is Paul's Christ-Wisdom.

---

1 George Eldon Ladd, *A Theology of the New Testament* (Grand Rapids: Eerdmans, 1974), pp. 419-421; see also Oscar Cullmann, *The Christology of the New Testament* (Philadelphia: Westminster Press, 1973), pp. 166-181; Ethelbert Stauffer, *New Testament Theology* (London: SCM Press, 1963), pp. 117-118; Herman Ridderbos, *Paul: An Outline of his Theology* (Grand Rapids: Eerdmans, 1975), pp. 73-75.

This Logos is also the agent of creation: "Nothing mortal can be made in the likeness of the Most High One and Father of the Universe, but only in that of the second God, who is his Logos." He is "the head of all things" (*Quaest.*, Ex. 2, 117). But the Logos is also the Primal Man: "There is however another Man, made in God's image, the archetype of Man." "The heavenly Man being the eternal archetype of mankind, is therefore Logos, and as such the first-born Son of God." The earthly Adam was a creation corresponding to him, but the heavenly Man was neither created nor uncreated, but somewhere in between.[1]

Next to be considered are examples from literature from farther afield than John and Philo, but C.H. Dodd thinks that they stem from the same Jewish atmosphere of speculations.[2] The Naassenes believed in a Primal Man who was to be identified with the Logos.[3] Also, the Hermetic tract *Poimandres* at least associates the Word of God with the Man, who is the Father's own image. As with the pre-human Christ of Philippians, he is also described in terms of the "form" ($\mu o\rho\phi\eta$) of God. He has creative power, though the role of agency is primarily associated with the Word and the Demiurge.[4] Much later Jewish mystical speculation also shows the conceptual viability of combining the idea of the Primal Man with attributes of Wisdom. Isaac Luria's 16th century Kabbalism describes the heavenly Man, Adam Kadmon, as embracing the world within himself, functioning in the ordering of the elements, and bearing the image of God in the sense that his universe-filling limbs (cf., Eph. 4:10) represented the attributes of God.[5]

It seems fair on the basis of the above material to infer the existence of a well-defined concept of Adam/Wisdom, the image of God and agent

---

1 C.H. Dodd, *The Interpretation of the Fourth Gospel* (Cambridge at the University Press, 1953), pp. 70-71; see also Martin Hengel, *The Son of God* (Philadelphia: Fortress Press, 1976), p. 70.

2 Dodd, p. 111.

3 Dodd, p. 110.

4 Dodd, pp. 31-32.

5 Gershom Scholem, *Major Trends in Jewish Mysticism* (New York: Schocken Books, 1973), p. 269.

of creation. Paul, too, seems to use this picture in his theology. In fact, this concept would seem to supply the ontological category for Paul's pre-incarnational Christology. Traditional Christian theology, however, has spoken of the incarnation of God. Is this justified in light of Paul's pre-incarnational concepts? Or would Paul have made the same point the same way? Two things are immediately evident from the preceding survey of Wisdom/Primal Man motifs. First, Wisdom was generally thought of as having been created at some point, or at least somehow not eternally pre-existent. Second, Wisdom, Logos, etc., can be described in some sense as "God." Philo called the Logos "a second God;" John calls the Logos "God" (John 1:1) and "the only-begotten God" (1:18). As already noted, Paul preserves the first of these two ideas in his conception of the pre-human Christ, but what about the second? Was this being considered "God"? Perhaps a brief survey of the texts where Paul seems to designate Christ as "God" will help suggest an answer.

The clearest text on this matter is Romans 9:5.[1] While the doxology in this verse might conceivably refer to God the Father, the wording makes this unnatural and unlikely. The form makes it an appositional doxology, liked those addressed to God the Father in Romans 1:25 and 2 Corinthians 11:31. But here the subject is Christ.[2] In discussing the divine favors given Israel, Paul mentions that, "of their race, according to the flesh, is the Christ, who is God over all." Various considerations indicate that "God over all" is a title only of the risen/exalted Christ. First, in Philippians 2:9-11, Paul says that at Christ's exaltation he was given the divine name, "Lord" with all of its divine honors (cf., vv. 10-11 with Isa. 45:23). Before the incarnation he had not been God's equal (see above). Similarly, in Romans 1:4, it is said that Jesus was constituted Son of God at the resurrection. There is a significant parallel between Romans 1:4 and 9:5. In both, Paul first recalls Jesus' human origin and natural heritage ("descended from David according to the flesh"/"of their race according to the flesh") and then describes

---

1 See the discussion of these and the following passages in Vincent Taylor, "Does the New Testament Call Jesus 'God'?" In Taylor, *New Testament Essays* (Grand Rapids: Eerdmans, 1972), pp. 84-87.

2 Cullmann, pp. 312-313.

his heavenly status ("Son of God"/"God over all"). The parallel would suggest that in both cases the second status is chronologically subsequent to the first, first entered upon via the resurrection/exaltation. This is further supported by the form of the title "God over all." This is analogous to Christ being "head over all things" (Eph. 1:22), a position bestowed on him, as the context shows, at the resurrection/exaltation. This title would also parallel the ascended Christ being "Lord of all" (Acts 1:36; cf., 2:36). However, it should be noted that the same sort of title can occur with reference to Christ's mediating role at creation. He is "head of all rule and authority" apparently because it was all created through him and for him (Col. 2:10 and 1:16), just as Philo could refer to the heavenly Logos as "the head of all things" (*Quaest.*, Ex. 2, 117).

Even in the Colossians passage, however, it is legitimate to ask if all things were created "for him" precisely in view of his destined exaltation (cf., Heb. 1:2 and 4, where Christ is heir at creation but actually inherits at his exaltation). This kind of notion may be in view in Colossians 2:15. In light of the Pauline (and general early Christian) picture of Christ gaining heavenly authority at his exaltation, it seems most likely that Romans 9:5 is to be understood as a reference only to the exalted Christ. Christ as cosmocrator may be called "God over all" even as Satan may be described as "the god of this world" (2 Cor. 4:4). That such a bestowal of the divine name is not inconsistent with Jewish monotheism is evident in the later apocalypse 3 Enoch, where the exalted and transfigured Enoch is christened "the Lesser Yahweh." Also, according to some rabbinic traditions, the Messiah would bear the name Yahweh.[1]

The only other Pauline (?) text which seems to call Christ "God" is Titus 2:13: "[We are] awaiting our blessed hope, the appearing of the glory of our great God and Savior, Jesus Christ." The text is to be translated so as to apply both titles to Jesus Christ in view of the indivisibility of "God and Savior" in the Pastoral Epistles (1 Tim. 1:1; 2:3; 4:10; Titus 1:3; 2:10; 3:4). Also, 1 Timothy 6:16 states that God

---

1 Philip B. Harner, *The "I Am" of the Fourth Gospel* (Philadelphia: Fortress Press, 1970), p. 25.

(the Father) can never be seen, so that it is unlikely that it is he who is said in this passage to be "appearing."[1] As for the text itself, it occurs in a clearly eschatological setting, and it may be that Christ is here called "our God" in his capacity as exalted and returning Lord. He will appear to crush the last pockets of resistance, after which he will abdicate his Lordship (1 Cor. 15:24-25). In a similar context, the Qumran Melchizedek midrash[2] describes the victorious Parousia of the warrior angel Melchizedek at the End to destroy the forces of evil. The mighty deliverer is unabashedly called "God."

Second Thessalonians 1:12 has been taken as attributing the title "God" to Christ, but this seems unlikely. Only one article is used (κατα την χαριν του Θεου ημω ν και κυριου Ιησου Χριστω), but this need not mean that only one person is being spoken of. The same construction occurs in 2 Corinthians 1:2 (χαριξ υμιν και ειρηνη απο Θεου πατρος ημων και κυριου Ιη σου Χριστου). It is hardly likely that Paul means to equate Jesus Christ with God the Father as the same person.[3] Also, the sentence in 1 Thessalonians 1:12 with its mention of grace seems to hark back to 1:2, where grace is associated with Christ and the Father as separate persons. Two sentences seem parallel, so that 1:12 does not make Christ "God" any more than does 1:2.

Colossians 2:2, which mentions του Θεου Χριστου, far from making Christ "God," as some seem to hold, actually makes Christ the *mystery* of God, a concept perhaps akin to that of the Wisdom of God. First Timothy 3:16 according to some manuscripts describes the incarnation as follows: "God was manifested in the flesh," but this is almost certainly an easily explicable textual corruption, Θεος being substituted for Ος ("Who").

The evidence, then, does not suggest that Paul considered the Godhood of Christ to extend back into his pre-human existence. But does

---

1 Cullmann, pp. 313-314.

2 Geza Vermes, *The Dead Sea Scrolls in English* (Baltimore: Penguin Books, 1975), pp. 266-268.

3 Cullmann, p. 313.

the resultant picture of his pre-incarnational Christology at least allow that he *might* have regarded the pre-human Christ as "God" even if he happened never to have explicitly said so? It has already been noted that both John and Philo felt they could designate the Word as "God." Their concept of the Word is otherwise very similar to Paul's picture of Christ-Wisdom. A brief look at the Johannine Christology might indicate the possibilities of these parallels shedding further light on Pauline Christology.

For John as well as Paul the pre-incarnate Christ was begotten or made alive (1:4; 6:57) at some point prior to the rest of creation, of which in turn he is the agent (1:3). The Word becomes flesh (1:4) just as the heavenly Man exchanged the form of God for the form of a servant (Phil. 2:6-7). On earth, Jesus looks forward to the time when he will be invested with honor equal to that of the Father, along with the divine prerogative of judgment (5:22-23). But until this exaltation, the Son is not as great as the Father (14:28). After the exaltation, Jesus is to be addressed as "Lord" and "God" (20:28). So far, the parallel is pretty close, but John, of course, calls the pre-incarnate Word "God" as well (1:1, 18). Why did Paul refrain from doing this? It seems he might as well have done it. As hinted earlier, the title "God" seems to be used functionally in a variety of ways. The (messianic?) king (Psalm 45:6; Isa.9:6), human judges (Psalm 82:6, on some interpretations), Melchizedek, Satan, and Christ as cosmocrator may all be designated "God." Jesus himself seems to have been reminding his opponents of this flexibility in John 10:34-36.

It seemed to Paul that the title "God over all" was appropriate for the exalted Christ. But it apparently did not occur to him to give the title to the pre-incarnate Christ-Wisdom. Perhaps this was because he was so taken with the exalted glory of the risen Christ that he did not want to risk confusing issues by calling Christ "God" at an earlier stage. A similar reservation seems to have been exercised by the Writer to the Hebrews. The pre-existent Christ is described by him as the agent of creation (1:2) and is characterized in terms of Wisdom in the Wisdom of Solomon (Heb. 1:3). However, Christ is "crowned with glory and honor" (2:9) only after his suffering (cf., Luke 24:26). He then inherits "all things," which had been made through him (1:2), obtaining the divine name, which is above the angels (1:4), namely "God" (1:8) or "Lord" (1:10). The context here is one of anointing (1:9), enthronement (1:13), and "crowning" (2:9). Before the incarnation, he was divine Wisdom, but only after the exaltation is he to be called "God." But as we have seen, John did not feel the need to make such a distinction. Thus the difference is more semantical than theological. Or, to put it another way, the theological differences are not ultimately contradictions. Paul apparently did not think of the pre-existent Christ as "God," but he could have easily enough, within the conceptual thought-world of his Christology. It all depends on what one means by "God."

<h2 style="text-align:center">APPENDIX:
ON THE QUESTION OF
CHRISTOLOGICAL SHIBBOLETHS</h2>

Of course, quite a lot depends on what one means by "God," especially with regard to issues of Christology. Lurking, scarcely hidden, beneath the surface of the preceding discussion have been questions such as the eternality of Christ, the meaning of the "deity" of Christ, and the Trinity itself. The line of interpretation pursued in this study has tended toward what might be called Arian or Adoptionist conclusions. This is so especially insofar as it stresses the dependence of Pauline Christology on the concept of Wisdom as the created agent of creation, and insofar as the deity of Christ is interpreted along the lines of deification. If these suggestions for interpreting Pauline Christology are correct, then at least the Trinitarian demand for the eternal pre-existence of Christ is misguided, and not merely a later development of implicit ideas.[1] And if the suggestion as to the ambiguous, functional nature of the title "God" is correct, this further raises a question mark beside the necessity of a doctrine of the Trinity. The Trinity is really just a name for an enigma of three co-eternal persons as one God, not an explanation of it. But if the present suggestions are correct, the usage of the

---

1　As Arthur W. Wainwright suggests in his *The Trinity in the New Testament* (London: SPCK, 1975), pp. 264-267.

title "God" need not necessarily imply all the ontological predicates which seem to require the enigmatic doctrine of the Trinity.

The formulations of the Christological councils are accepted and maintained by "Sola Scriptura" Protestants on the basis of the contention that these creeds are directly grounded in, or at least continuous with, the teaching of the New Testament (whereas it seems more likely the product of a reluctance to depart from the very ecclesiastical tradition against which Protestants would like to consider themselves liberated). But if such uninterrupted continuity cannot in fact be shown, can the creeds still be binding? If one reverts instead to the bare New Testament text, the boundaries of Christological orthodoxy seem to widen. The shibboleths are not so subtle. In the first place, more diversity will be allowed, since the New Testament writers show diversity among themselves,[1] as already shown here. And since their writings are canonical, whatever they say will *ipso facto* be orthodox. But even when one examines their writings to see what, if anything, was uniformly forbidden for Christian belief, the resulting "rule of faith" is not so complicated as traditional theology would make it.

John 4:2-3 forbids docetism. Paul no doubt would agree, since it was important to him that the Son of God be a sharer of human flesh, so as to defeat sin on its own ground (Rom. 8:3). John demands confession of Jesus as Son of God (1 John 4:15) and Christ (2:22), just as Paul required confession of Jesus as Lord (Rom. 10:9-1). Paul also listed as essential elements of belief the death, burial, and resurrection of Jesus (1 Cor. 15:1-2ff; Rom. 10:9-10). In fact, soteriology rather than details of Christology seems to have marked the great dividing line for Paul. Those who advocate the necessity of the Law for salvation have stultified the death of Christ (Gal. 2:21; 3:1) and in fact preach a different (i.e., counterfeit) gospel and Jesus (Gal. 1:6-7; 2 Cor. 11:4). There may be an element of flexibility even here, however, since Paul did not anathematize James and the Jerusalem Christians who felt that the Law was binding upon Jewish Christians (Acts 21:20-25). Also,

---

1 Ernst Käsemann, "The Canon of the New Testament and the Unity of the Church." In Käsemann, *Essays on New Testament Themes*. Studies in Biblical Theology No. 41 (London: SCM Press, 1960), pp. 95-107.

apostles of legalism may be in view in Philippians 1:15 and 16 as in 3:2ff, yet Paul rejoices that these trouble-makers at least preach Christ (1:18). Of course, he might mean that even false preaching of Christ helped spread the word of why he, Paul, is imprisoned, since it generates more talk about the gospel (cf., 1:12-13).[1] In general, however, a Jesus whose death still leaves the need for one's own saving efforts is a different Jesus. Partisans of this Christ are no real Christians (Gal. 1:8-9; 2 Cor. 11:13-15).

Whatever may have been the full Christological theology of the New Testament writers, their explicit statements as to the limits of orthodox belief seem to boil down to the following picture: Jesus was a truly human being. He died, was buried, and rose from the dead. His death is sufficient for salvation and requires no supplement. He now reigns as Lord and is Christ and God's Son.[2] It is perhaps unfair to extract a "lowest common denominator" from the New Testament since the writings are so obviously occasional and therefore fragmentary, not containing everything their writers believed about any given topic. Also, it is hard to imagine the apostolic writers allowing that one could be content with some kind of "mere Christianity" if they believed and taught a fuller picture themselves.

Nonetheless, if modern Christians felt that they could rest content with the (meager) Christological shibboleths outlined by the New Testament writers, the name "Christian" might be charitably allowed to some who are now stigmatized as heretical over some philosophical refinement or other. Perhaps Paul's advice might profitably be taken: "Accept him whose faith is weak, without passing judgment on disputable matters" (Rom. 14:1).

---

1 "There's no such thing as bad publicity."

2 James D.G. Dunn, in his *Unity and Diversity in the New Testament* (Philadelphia: Westminster Press, 1977), arrives at a very similar, though even more modest, shared core of New Testament belief.

The Austerity Gospel of Gordon Fee

I am a grateful student of Gordon Fee, having studied with him from 1974 through 1978.[1] He is a fine biblical scholar and a keen and powerful preacher. Theologically, he calls himself a "Presbycostal," because, though committed to his home denomination of the Assemblies of God, he long ago embraced basic aspects of Calvinist, Reformed theology. Most Pentecostals tend to be theologically Arminian, so he is unusual, but there is no inconsistency in his position, and his hybrid views attest his independent thinking. Despite, or rather *because* of, his Pentecostal orientation, Fee takes a very dim view of certain prominent aspects of today's Charismatic Movement (which overlaps the Pentecostal denominations while not being simply synonymous with them).

Specifically, Fee detests and disdains the Prosperity Gospel. I want to summarize his objections as put forward in his succinct booklet, *The Disease of the Health & Wealth Gospels.*[2] It will become evident that, while I have very serious disagreements with my old mentor's reasoning, I think his main contention is right on target.

[T]he bottom line... always comes back to one continual reaffirmation: God *wills* the (financial) prosperity of every one of his children, and therefore for a Christian to be in poverty is to be outside God's intended will; it is to be living a Satan-defeated life... Because we are

---

1 Not that it makes any difference, but for the record, I first sat under Fee's teaching at a college youth retreat in 1974, which led me to seek him out at Gordon-Conwell Theological Seminary, where he became my academic advisor. I took courses with him between 1976 and 1978.

2 Gordon D. Fee, *The Disease of the Health & Wealth Gospels* (Costa Mesa: The Word for Today, 1979).

God's children, the King's kids, as some like to put it, we should always go first-class—we should have the biggest and best, a Cadillac instead of a Volkswagen, because this alone brings glory to God (a curious theology indeed given the nature of the Incarnation and the Crucifixion). But these affirmations are not biblical, no matter how much one might clothe them in biblical garb. (p. 3)

Fee aims his guns at Evangelical Charismatics, not at New Thought Christians. There are significant points of difference, e.g., in terms of God-concept, Christology, and biblical interpretation, as we will see. But much or most of his argument is applicable to both camps. Remember, the Prosperity Gospel espoused by prominent Evangelical TV preachers is the result of an earlier generation of Pentecostals, influenced by Charismatic Baptist E. W. Kenyon, having embraced New Thought doctrines.[1]

THE BIBLE AS VENTRILOQUIST DUMMY

Fee is first and foremost a New Testament specialist, dedicated to the determination of authorial intent in every Bible passage. If one esteems the Bible a source of inspired and authoritative teaching,[2] one must try to determine what the author was trying to convey. And in this Prosperity preachers appear to have little interest. "The most distressing thing about their use of scripture... is the purely subjective and arbitrary way they interpret the biblical text." (p. 3)

There is a small set of scripture passages to which Prosperity Gospel teachers regularly appeal, and Fee cannot shut his ears to the screaming of the texts at the abuse they are forced to undergo. The most important is 3 John, verse 2, usually (and conveniently) cited in the archaic and easily misunderstood King James Version: "Beloved, I wish

---

1 D.R. McConnell, *A Different Gospel* (Peabody: Hendrickson Publications, 1995).

2 There are, of course, other roles that scripture plays in different types of theology. See David H. Kelsey, *The Uses of Scripture in Recent Theology* (Philadelphia: Fortress Press, 1975).

above all things that thou mayest prosper and be in health, even as thy soul prospereth." A*ha*! See *that*? The Bible says you ought to be prosperous! Uh, not so fast!

> This combination of wishing for "things to go well" and for the recipient's "good health" was the *standard* form of greeting in a personal letter in antiquity. To extend John's wish for Gaius [the addressee of 3 John] to refer to financial and material prosperity for all Christians of all times is *totally foreign* to the text… We may as well argue that all subsequent Christians are out of God's will who do not go to Carpus's house in Troy in order to take Paul's cloak to him (2 Tim. 4:13). (p. 4)

Appeal to 3 John 2 in this manner is tantamount to superstitious incantation. Fee is right. Nor is this the only such text pressed into service for the Gospel of Wealth. Another is John 10:10, "I came that they might have life and have it more abundantly." Did somebody say "abundance"? As in wealth? "What's in *your* wallet?"

> It should be noted further that "abundant life" in John 10:10, the second important text of this movement, also has nothing to do with material abundance… The Greek word *perrison*, translated "more abundantly" in the KJV, means simply that believers are to enjoy this gift of life "to the full" (NIV). [Fee explains the Johannine connotation of "life" as "eternal life," "divine life," i.e., saving grace.] Material abundance is not implied either in the word "life" or "to the full." Furthermore, such an idea is totally foreign to the context of John 10. (p. 5)

Once Prosperity preachers opportunistically rip these verses out of context, they employ them as a lens through which to view (i.e., to distort) all others. Fee takes Kenneth Copeland to task: for Copeland to take the Rich Young Ruler story (Mark 10:17-22) to mean that "Jesus is affirming his wealth as the result of his lifelong obedience, and was only testing him to give it away, so that he might regain all the more… is… plainly contrary to the *intent* of the text" (p. 5). Indeed, one cannot keep from cringing. Such an interpretation "is almost totally subjective, and comes not from study but from 'meditation,' which in

Copeland's case means a kind of free association based on a prior commitment to his—totally wrong—understanding of the 'basic' texts" (pp. 5-6). Here the Bible has become little more than a Rorschach ink blot test.

New Thought Christians may not handle biblical interpretation in precisely the same way as Copeland and his colleagues, but I think Fee's rebuke applies to them as well. Insofar as the allegorical method is used in service of the New Thought version of the Prosperity Gospel it, too, discards the criterion of authorial intent. This may not seem to be the same sin committed by Copeland, Kenneth Hagin and the rest, since New Thought disavows the biblicism, the biblical literalism, these men claim to embrace. But the result is the same: biblical ventriloquism. The purpose of allegory, whether applied to the *Iliad* and the *Odyssey* or the Bible, is to make bad texts look good, to render useless texts useful, by pretending they say something other than what they do say. And this means making the texts seem to parrot our doctrines, which we proceed to read *into* them, not *out of* them.

DOES GOD PLAY FAVORITES?

Does the Bible really leave one with the impression that the life of piety is the secret of prosperity and worldly success? I think it is fair to say that Deuteronomy and the Deuteronomic History (Joshua-Judges-Samuel-Kings) based on it do point in that direction. The Moses character presents Israel with a list of blessings promised by Jehovah if the nation upholds the statutes of the Covenant, along with a table of curses (misfortunes) if they don't. But this impression is mitigated somewhat once we realize that the whole thing is actually a centuries-after-the-fact *theodicy*. That is, this "Deuteronomic philosophy of history" is a contrived and artificial fabrication designed to get the Almighty off the hook for apparently abandoning Israel and Judah to the depredations of their Assyrian and Babylonian conquerors. "Gee, I guess it must have been *our* fault, huh? Otherwise, we'd have to blame God, and that's even worse."[1]

---

1 Fee would never see the Deuteronomic History as tendentious fiction; he

Some point to Job as an example of an upright man amply rewarded by God for his perfect piety. If God could reward *him* with extravagant fringe benefits, why not *us*? And the whole membership of the Full Gospel Businessmen's Fellowship? Uh, keep reading! The whole point of the Book of Job seems to be that the righteous need *not* expect God's blessing and protection, and that they may never know why. *Ouch.* Just the opposite of any Prosperity Gospel, one would think.

Fee points out that Luke 13:1-5 assures us that the rain and the sunshine fall upon just and unjust alike,[1] while Hebrews 11:32-39 cites Old Testament figures who were faithful and yet did not receive any reward, even any vindication, in this life. Hebrews 10:34 speaks of believers acquiescing in the seizure of their property in times of persecution, i.e., *because* they were righteous (p. 7). From all this, my old mentor derives what I call his "austerity gospel," the "good news" that Christians should drop prosperity from their agendas and expectations.

Here, however, one must suspect that Fee is making the exception *into* the rule: must Christians be so paranoid as to expect, even *provoke*, constant persecution, martyrdom as a "life"-style? In the same way, might the New Testament admonitions to renounce one's possessions have this very circumstance (an atypical one) in view: persecution? Walter Schmithals[2] thought so. Thus Luke 14:33 and similar passages might be analogous to Luke 14:26-27 which urges Christians to "hate" their families, i.e., to turn a deaf ear to their pleas to save oneself from martyrdom by renouncing one's faith (as in *The Martyrdom*

---

is too much of a conservative Evangelical for that. But I think this more critical approach underlines his broader point.

1 Though I can see Prosperity Gospel fans pointing to James 5:16b-18 as implying that God's favorites can control the weather as they prefer by means of prayer!

2 Walter Schmithals, *The Theology of the First Christians*. Trans. O.C. Dean, Jr. (Louisville: Westminster John Knox Press, 1997), p. 346: "Luke's paraenesis [hortatory instruction] regarding poverty and possessions is directed toward Christians who are oppressed by the experience of persecution."

of Perpetua and Felicitas). The everyday Christian life would hardly be in view here. Schmithals says, "Thus what was recommended to [e.g.,] the disenfranchised Matthean churches as realistic behavior in the concrete historical situation of persecution… would be grossly misunderstood as a timeless principle of ethical behavior."[1] But that is precisely how Fee understands these passages. It is tantamount to telling all Christians it *is* their permanent duty to retrieve Paul's cloak from Carpus' house.

Fee outlines his alternative view of biblical teaching, one diametrically opposed to that of proponents of the Success Gospel.

In the full biblical view wealth and possessions are a zero value for the people of God. … Poverty, however, is *not* seen to be better. If God has revealed Himself as the One who pleads the cause of the poor… He is not thereby blessing poverty. Rather, He is revealing His mercy and justice in behalf of those whom the wealthy regularly oppress in order to get, or maintain, their wealth. (p. 7)

This carefree attitude toward wealth and possessions, for which *neither* prosperity *nor* poverty is a value, is thoroughgoing in the New Testament. According to Jesus, the good news of the inbreaking of the Kingdom frees us from all those pagan concerns (Matt. 6:32). With His own coming the Kingdom has been inaugurated—even though it has yet to be fully consummated; the time of God's rule is now; the future with its new values is already at work in the present… In the new order, brought about by Jesus, the standard is sufficiency; and surplus is called into question. The one with two tunics should share with him who has none (Luke 3:11);[2] "possessions" are to be sold and given to the poor (Luke 12:33)… Therefore, if one has possessions, prexcisely because they have no inherent value, he can freely share them with the needy. But if one does not have possessions, he is not to seek them. God cares for one's needs; the extras are unnecessary; the rich man who seeks more and more is a fool; life does not consist in having a surplus of possessions (Luke 12:15). (pp. 7-8)

---

1 Schmithals, p. 345.

2 Though, technically, that's John the Baptist talking, not Jesus.

It is no surprise to see Fee conclude: "The cult of prosperity thus flies full in the face of the whole New Testament. It is not biblical in any sense" (p. 9).

IT'S A FEE, NOTHING,
FEE, NOTHING, FEE, NOTHING MORE[1]

I regret to say that I have several objections to Fee's alternative view of the "true" gospel message. First, I believe that he unwittingly espouses the very notion he repudiates, namely that God does not prefer poverty to prosperity. The "mercy and justice" he is so sure God will exercise on behalf of the righteous poor is not likely to be in evidence on this side of the grave. *Great.* Fee promises no one seventy-two virgins waiting in Paradise, true, but ultimately, what's the difference? Eschatological goodies: "I want a mansion just over the hilltop in that bright land where we'll never grow old." But until then, we're stuck chewing the stale crusts of pious austerity, mere sufficiency. In my book, that's just another name for poverty.

The further one reads, the clearer it becomes that Fee, along with many of his more "sophisticated" contemporary Evangelicals, has embraced an inexcusably naïve Christian Socialism (if not actual Anarcho-Syndicalism). He disdains the Prosperity message as

> an Americanized perversion of the Gospel [which] tends to reinforce a way of life and an economic system that repeatedly oppresses the poor... Seeking more prosperity means to support all the political and economic programs that have made such prosperity available—but almost always at the expense of economically deprived individuals and nations. (pp. 10-11)

Socialism has impoverished every society where it has been adopted. In economic matters, Fee is happy to walk by faith, not by sight.[2]

---

1 Tim Rice, "Damned for All Time/Blood Money." In *Jesus Christ Superstar* (Universal City: MCA, 1970).

2 I call this sort of "faith" politics "political snake-handling." Obey what

Socialism looks good to him or to anyone else only because of the failure to understand that one need not cut ever-thinner slices of the pie for everyone to get some, because Capitalism makes it possible to increase the size of the pie.

I think I see Fee's Pentecostalism showing itself here. Just as Pentecostals reject Bultmann's demythologizing,[1] insisting that we still inhabit the ancient world of spirits, demons, and miracles, Fee stubbornly retains the ancient belief in the "limited good," the notion that there is only so much supply to go around, so that if anyone is wealthy, it must be because he has deprived the poor of their fair share.[2] That was true in the ancient and medieval world, before Capitalism, before industrial and modern agricultural production. Now there is something new under the sun: an affluent middle class. But for liberals, it is not good enough that many or most can be affluent. No, if there are *any* poor, the whole thing is unjust. Better that everyone live with less than that some have more than others. If universal poverty is the price of universal equality, so be it.[3]

We have seen that Fee rejects the belief that God rewards his darlings with prosperity. I think that, unfortunately, Fee is consistent

---

(you think) the Bible says and let the chips fall where they may! For Christian Science believers and "Doctor Jesus" Pentecostals, it can mean trashing your child's insulin; for Fee, Ron Sider, and their fellows, it means collapsing the American consumer economy. Jim Wallis once admitted to me he thought the collapse of our economy would be a good thing.

1 Rudolf Bultmann, "New Testament and Mythology." Trans. Reginald H. Fuller. In Hans Werner Bartsch, ed., *Kerygma and Myth: A Theological Debate* (New York: Harper & Row, 1961), pp. 1-44.

2 Bruce J. Malina, *The New Testament World: Insights from Cultural Anthropology* (Atlanta: John Knox Press, 1981), Chapter 4, "The Perception of Limited Good," pp. 71-93.

3 Fee insists that his readers run right out and get a copy of Ron Sider's leftist screed *Rich Christians in an Age of Hunger*. I would suggest that, when they finish Sider, they take a look at David Chilton's counter-blast *Productive Christians in an Age of Guilt Manipulators*. (Okay, Chilton is a Christian Reconstructionist nut, but he's right about Sider.)

in applying the same attitude to modern economics. Like all Social-ists, Fee seems to deny that industrious, and thus successful, people should be rewarded. We can see the disastrous results of this absur-dity in the policies of the present Obama administration. So, for Fee, the Kingdom teaching of Jesus *does* mandate poverty as a virtue.

DECONSTRUCTING FEE'S AUSTERITY GOSPEL

Gordon Fee's wide and deep scholarship seems to me to be hampered and hamstrung by his conservative Evangelical doctrine of an inspired and infallible Bible. It gives him an irresistible tendency to harmonize all opinions found in the Bible into a single normative "biblical theol-ogy," which he uses to browbeat the Prosperity Gospel. But I think it is not so simple. I think Fee unwittingly synthesizes three distinct so-cio-ethical perspectives found in different strata of the canonical New Testament. Combining them, Fee produces a Chimera, a hybrid beast that, like a mule (which combines the genes of a horse and a donkey), is sterile.

First, there is the apocalyptic business about the "inbreaking of the Kingdom of God." Fee has embraced the understanding of gospel es-chatology developed by scholars of the post-World War II generation, including Joachim Jeremias, Oscar Cullmann, Rudolf Bultmann,[1] Günter Bornkamm,[2] and Norman Perrin.[3] The idea was that Jesus proclaimed that the Kingdom of God (entailing the Final Judgment, the banishment of all worldly regimes, and the resurrection of the dead) was so soon to dawn that the first rays of it could already be seen and felt, beginning to illumine the spiritual and moral darkness of the fallen, Satan-ruled world. These first signs of the Kingdom's arrival were the miraculous healings and exorcisms performed by Je-

---

1 Rudolf Bultmann, *Jesus and the Word*. Trans. Louise Pettibone Smith and Erminie Huntress Lantero (New York: Scribners, 1958).

2 Günter Bornkamm, *Jesus of Nazareth*. Trans. Irene and Fraser McLuskey with James M. Robinson (New York: Harper & Row, 1960).

3 Norman Perrin, *The Kingdom of God in the Teaching of Jesus*. New Testa-ment Library (London: SCM Press, 1963).

sus through the power of the Holy Spirit.[1] Reminiscent of Gandhi's dictum, "Be the change you wish to see," Jesus' teachings in the Sermon on the Mount, the parables, etc., urged his hearers to live by the standards appropriate to the Millennial era already in the (short-lived) present. This constituted an ethos of indifference toward material possessions, the willingness to love and forgive, the sharing of resources with the poor, etc. Those living such a life among one's brothers and sisters would be getting a head start on the eschatological Kingdom.

DEBACLE-YPSE NOW

In case you haven't glanced at the calendar lately, the eschatological hope failed to materialize. Mark 9:1 and 13:30 set a time-frame for the end of the present age. It must take place within the generation of Jesus' contemporaries. But even without such an explicit deadline, the time-frame was implicit in the urgent appeal to repent given the near approach of the Eschaton. Unlike today's desperate fundamentalists, who twist the texts in order to deny that Jesus set a deadline, Fee's mentors freely admitted there had been a surprising (i.e., embarrassing) delay of some *two thousand years*. Cullmann[2] sought to make sense of this by using the analogy of D Day and V-E Day, still fresh in the minds of his readers. Once the D Day invasion occurred, the outcome of the European war was no longer in doubt. The Nazi regime was doomed. But that didn't mean the war was over there and then. No, there was still a long and difficult "mopping-up operation" ahead. That continued until V-E Day, Victory in Europe Day. That's when the parades started. Cullmann said that the death and resurrection of Jesus marked the decisive turning-point of D Day, and that the Second Coming would be V-E Day, the final triumph of Christ. Jeremias[3] called this schema

---

1 Reginald H. Fuller, *Interpreting the Miracles* (London: SCM Press, 1963), pp. 39-42.

2 Oscar Cullmann, *Christ and Time: The Primitive Christian Conception of Time and History*. Trans. Floyd V. Filson (Philadelphia: Westminster Press, 1950), p. 84. In the classroom, Fee would regularly use Cullmann's analogy.

3 Joachim Jeremias, *New Testament Theology*. Trans. John Bowden (London:

"inaugurated eschatology" or "eschatology in the process of realizing itself." In the meantime, the Church, the Christian community, functions as the embattled beach head of the Kingdom in the midst of its doomed foes. Fee locates the radical ethics of discipleship in that isolated Christian colony amid the blasted heath of Satan's kingdom.

This is all quite ingenious, but I do not think it can survive the two-millennia-long delay of the Kingdom. Albert Schweitzer[1] understood why. The extreme character of "Kingdom ethics" made sense only on the (now-failed) assumption of an early Second Advent. To take but one example, one is both free to and obliged to give one's possessions to the poor precisely because there is not going to be any earthly future to keep them in reserve for. Very soon there will be no need for financial resources, savings, provisions. The redeemed and resurrected will dine on the roasted Leviathan and the bread of angels at the Marriage Supper of the Lamb. Money will be worthless, like Confederate dollars after the Civil War. In the last days before the soon-coming end, it is good for one thing only: to feed the desperate poor who are still hungry during the short interval remaining. Which you'd damn well better do if you hope to prove yourself worthy to survive the Final Judgment. In ordinary circumstances no one blames you for not giving all your savings to feed the poor since you're going to need the money to feed your family and send your kids to college. But if the end is at hand, your priorities suddenly change. Schweitzer called this the "interim ethic" of Jesus.

But suppose no Kingdom comes. You're left holding the bag. Just like all the poor fools who spent their savings on billboards announcing the end of the world on October 21, 2011, as Harold Camping predicted. Yikes! I guess you and your fellow disappointed zealots can huddle together and pool the little cash you've got left and hope you can make ends meet till the Kingdom *does* arrive some day (fingers crossed!). Then, congratulations, you have become a sectarian conven-

---

SCM Press, 1971), Chapter III, section 11, "The Dawn of the Reign of God," pp. 96-108.

1 Albert Schweitzer, *The Mystery of the Kingdom of God: The Secret of Jesus' Messiahship and Passion*. Trans. Walter Lowrie (New York: Schocken Books, 1964), Chapter III, "The Preaching of the Kingdom," pp. 94-105.

ticle, reassuring yourself that the Kingdom *did* come in, er, a spiritual sense—or something. Sometimes the members of such a community will consistently embrace the ethics appropriate to life in the (imagined) Millennium, notably celibacy (Luke 20:34-36; 1 Cor. 7:1-2), and then it is doomed to perish by attrition, staving off the inevitable by the expedient of trying to recruit new members, a pretty neat trick with such a gospel! The Shaker sect is extinct for just this reason.

But if they don't, they'll have children and gradually return to the norms of "worldly" (i.e., conventionally religious) society. In Weber's and Troeltsch's[1] terms, a sect will have become a church. The best you can do to preserve the once-radical values is to accommodate them to real-world (i.e., this-worldly) conditions, what Paul Tillich[2] called the conditions of ambiguity, or of finitude. You have to try to approximate the original ethics as best you can. You have to grapple with "the relevance of an impossible ethical ideal" (Reinhold Niebuhr).[3] And if the Kingdom of God will not come to *you*, you'll have to be satisfied with coming to *it*, when you die and wing your way skyward. So the way I see it, Gordon Fee is trying to hold on to the Interim Ethic of an apocalyptic Jesus, though it does not fit the real world—any more than Pentecostal insistence on supernatural miracles does.

LONE WOLVES IN SHEEP'S CLOTHING

The second aspect of gospel ethics that Fee mixes into his recipe for radical discipleship is the ascetical regimen of the wandering "brethren" (3 John 5-7; Matt. 25:31-46), variously described by scholars as

1 William H. Swatos, Jr., "Church-Sect Theory." In Swatos, ed., *Encyclopedia of Religion and Society*. Hartford Institute for Religion Research, Hartford Seminary (Walnut Creek: Alta Mira Press, 1998). <hirr.hartsem.edu/ency/cstheory.htm>

2 Paul Tillich, *Systematic Theology II: Existence and the Christ* (Chicago: University of Chicago Press, 1957), pp. 4, 80, 131-133, 144, 162.

3 Reinhold Niebuhr, *An Interpretation of Christian Ethics* (New York: Meridian Books, 1956), Chapter 4, "The Relevance of an Impossible Ethical Ideal," pp. 97-123.

"itinerant charismatics" and "itinerant radicals."[1] On into the second century there was a class of wandering missionaries who circulated among the Christian communities teaching, prophesying, etc. They were nearly indistinguishable from the wandering Cynic philosophers and were often confused with them.[2] These were the Christians who preserved (and, we may suspect, *produced*) the Missionary Charge texts of the gospels (Mark 6:7-11; Matt. 10:5-23; Luke 9:1-6; 10:1-16). They pointed with pride to their radical itinerant lifestyle: they had actually left home, family, lands, and money to spread the word of Christ (Mark 10:28). Any who dared laugh off their thundered preachments would surely face the wrath of the Son of Man when he should come to wipe the snide smiles off their faces (Mark 8:38). Who but these strange, homeless scarecrows would ever have preserved sayings like Luke 14:26? Who else would have had an interest in admonishing Christians not to have dinner parties for their friends and family but instead to invite the poor and homeless (i.e., the holy itinerants themselves!), as in Luke 14:12-14? (Of course, the Rich Young Ruler story must have been a "discipleship paradigm," a recruiting story for the itinerants, who were "looking for a few good men.")

As Stevan L. Davies[3] recounts, these "apostles" eventually lost the support of the communities who gave them a meal and a night's shelter because they had less and less to say that was relevant to the increasingly bourgeoisie households and congregations to whom they sought to minister. Think of the Kafkaesque protagonist of the anonymous *The Way of a Pilgrim*, who wandered through Russia chanting the Jesus

---

1 Gerd Theissen, *Sociology of Early Palestinian Christianity*. Trans. John Bowden (Philadelphia: Fortress Press, 1978), pp. 8-30; Theissen, *Social Reality and the Early Christians: Theology, Ethics, and the World of the New Testament*. Trans. Margaret Kohl (Minneapolis: Fortress Press, 1992), Chapter 1, "The Wandering Radicals: Light Shed by the Sociology of Literature on the Early Transmission of Jesus Sayings," pp. 33-59.

2 F. Gerald Downing, *Cynics and Christian Origins* (Bloomsbury: T&T Clark, 2000).

3 Stevan L. Davies, *The Revolt of the Widows: The Social World of the Apocryphal Acts* (Carbondale: Southern Illinois University Press, 1980), p. 36.

Prayer. I think, too, of the sackcloth-clad Children of God who used to crash suburban church services, beating their wooden staves on the floors and rebuking the complacent pew-potatoes.[1]

Christian communities quickly found such "radical discipleship" eccentric, fanatical, and impracticable, as modern Christians do. We would cut these distressing verses from the gospels if we dared, but we can't, so most of us politely ignore them. But not Gordon Fee, who uses them as ingredients in his recipe for world-negating, poverty-inducing Christian Socialism. But it doesn't fit reality any better than it ever did.

AT EASE IN ZION

The gospels show an awareness of a third, separate ethic, this one for the settled Christian communities on whose support the itinerants depended. We are told to "give to him who asks of you" (Matt. 5:42), which inculcates a *habit* of generosity and philanthropy, but such advice makes no sense addressed to people who have repudiated all possessions in one fell swoop, as Jesus summons the Rich Young Ruler to do. Lazarus, Mary, and Martha (John 12:1-2) are not counted as sinners and villains for retaining enough money and property to provide charity and hospitality to an itinerant like Jesus! Had Mary Magdalene, Susanna, Joanna and the rest (Luke 8:1-3) simply dumped all they owned, they would not have been in the position to subsidize Jesus and his men in their travels, would they? And the talk about receiving a prophet's reward if one gives the prophet a glass of water (Matt. 10:41-42): surely the point of this is to buy good karma by subsidizing those who actually *have* embraced the rigorous discipline of the itinerant[2] (just as Bud-

---

1 Ronald M. Enroth, Edward E. Ericson, and C. Breckenridge Peters, *The Jesus People: Old-Time Religion in the Age of Aquarius* (Grand Rapids: Eerdmans, 1972), pp. 24, 34; Michael McFadden, *The Jesus Revolution* (New York: Harrow Books/Harper & Row, 1972), pp. 89-90; Daniel Cohen, *The New Believers: Young Religion in America* (New York: Ballantine Books, 1975), p. 6.

2 J. Duncan M. Derrett, "Financial Aspects of the Resurrection." In Robert M. Price and Jeffery Jay Lowder, eds., *The Empty Tomb: Jesus beyond the Grave* (Amherst: Prometheus Books, 2005), p. 397: "In that world the idea reigned

dhist laity donate food to the monks who go begging house to house).

Fee's synthesized "gospel of the Kingdom" fails by ignoring the serious difference between this more domesticated Christian ethic (on full display, for example, in the Pastoral Epistles) on the one hand and the apocalyptic Interim Ethic and the Dharma Bum regimen of the itinerant radicals on the other. Fee does not see the difference between the three varieties because of his conservative antipathy to form criticism which teaches us to bracket the editorial placement of originally isolated sayings into secondary narrative contexts.[1] Form-critical scrutiny reveals the three very different ethical models, and the different types of Christians for which they were originally intended. The harmonized hybrid Fee creates winds up holding settled, workaday Christian families responsible to keep heroic standards never intended for them. The result is just a new version of traditional, judgmental Christian browbeating, reinforcing hopeless guilt by imposing burdens the laity can never hope to bear (Luke 11:46; Acts 15:10).

CHARISMAGIC

I have leveled an array of serious criticisms against Gordon Fee's "austerity gospel" and the biblical basis he offers for it. But I cannot help thinking he is quite right in his most damning judgment on the Prosperity Gospel.

> Despite all protests to the contrary, at its base, the cult of prosperity offers a man-centered, rather than a God-centered theology. Even though one is regularly told that it is to God's own glory that we should prosper, the appeal is always made to our own selfishness and sense of wellbeing. (p. 10)

This seems to me hard to deny. The Evangelical version of the Prosperity Gospel espoused by preachers like Kenneth Copeland and Joel

---

that if one pays another to be righteous one becomes righteous oneself."

1 Rudolf Bultmann, *History of the Synoptic Tradition*. Trans. John Marsh (New York: Harper & Row, 1972), pp. 11, 39-40.

Osteen remains theistic. They still believe in a personal deity, and the result is that they reduce God to a servile genie eager to grant wishes. New Thought, on the other hand, has moved over to Monism and Pantheism, diffusing the deity into a mist of divine potentiality or distilling God into an impersonal set of supposed cosmic laws to be wielded unto the fulfilling of one's desires. This marks the retrogression of *religion* to *magic* as distinguished long ago by James Frazer.[1] As he understood the matter, magic is "occult science," the attempted effecting of boons by means of the supposed hidden laws implicit in the universe, no different in principle from the long-unsuspected forces and laws of physics. By contrast, religion is the adoration of invisible Persons of whom one humbly makes requests in prayer and sacrifice. The logic of religion is "Thy will be done," while that of magic is "My will be done." New Thought, as I understand it, falls into the latter category. There is no real God to worship. There is only the Force to manipulate. New Thought qualifies, in sociologist Bryan Wilson's terms, as a "gnostic-manipulationist sect." James C. Livingston (who lists Scientology and Transcendental Meditation under this rubric) defines such a sect this way:

> What is distinctive about this kind of group, sometimes called a cult, is the fact that it fully *accepts* and pursues what others would see as worldly goals. What it seeks is not withdrawal from or an indifference toward the world but, rather, appropriation of the right spiritual means or techniques by which to cope with [the world] or to achieve worldly goals. Salvation essentially means health, happiness, success, status, wealth, or long life.[2]

Don't get me wrong; I am all in favor of "visualization" and "manifesting" as means of achieving one's financial and material goals.[3] I just

---

1 See the discussion of Frazer's dichotomy in Mischa Titiev, "A Fresh Approach to the Problem of Magic and Religion." In William A. Lessa and Evon Z. Vogt, eds., *Reader in Comparative Religion: An Anthropological Approach* (New York: Harper & Row, 3rd ed., 1972), pp. 430-433.

2 James C. Livingston, *Anatomy of the Sacred: An Introduction to Religion* (New York: Macmillan, 1989), pp. 147-148.

3 Shakti Gawain, *Creative Visualization* (New York: Bantam Books, 1982).

think that to place these things in a religious or theological context confuses matters and risks cheapening religion. Remember, the Buddha remarked that, though praying to the traditional gods for rain and a good harvest might actually get you the desired results, none of that had a thing to do with liberation, the proper business of religion. I'm with Fee on that one.

Skepticism and Historical Method[1]

What I want to talk about today is skepticism and historical method. And what I want to try to show is *not* that skeptics use history to gain skeptical results: "Wouldn't it be great if we could prove that there is no God or that there was no Jesus? Let's come up with some method to show it." That would be axe grinding and propaganda. But some think that it is like that because they want the liberty to propose an alternative sort of "believing historical method," as it's sometimes called, or a "faithful historical method," but that is in the nature of the case impossible, and it's an error that underlies a lot of the stuff that I deal with in my reviews and books.

For instance, in a new book by Paul Eddy and Greg Boyd called *The Jesus Legend*—don't confuse it with G.A. Wells' *The Jesus Legend*—they take me to task quite often. I know and like these guys, I don't mean to just attack them, but they give it to me, and I think they're just wrong, wrong, wrong, and one thing they cannot get straight is that historical critics of the Bible do not begin with naturalistic philosophical assumptions—not that there's anything wrong with such assumptions if you happen to hold them. I tend to be agnostic on such things, in that a twerp like me could never hope to understand what's really going on in the universe. The idea is absurd; how can I ever know such a thing? But I do know what conceptual tools you have to use to do history, and they involve methodological atheism. As if you didn't understand, I want to take a little time explaining why that is, why there isn't any room to entertain a serious possibility of divine intervention and miracles having occurred in the past, and that this does not involve a dogmatic belief that they cannot have happened.

I like very much and I've remembered for many years the section in

---

1 A lecture given at Skepticon 2 Redux in November 2009.

Paul Tillich's book *Dynamics of Faith* in which he discusses doubt or skepticism. He said that three kinds of doubt have to be distinguished, especially when it comes to religion. There is what I guess he would call *constitutional* or *attitudinal* doubt where someone is just cynical or despairing of the truth to the degree that they become indifferent to finding it. They just don't think you can ever know, and so, what's the point? It would be good to know the truth if we could, but we probably can't, so the heck with it. But he says that even that has an element of faith, faith in the truth, that there is such a thing as the truth, whether or not you can arrive at it.

There's also *existential* doubt where you have committed yourself to some great cause or notion—some ultimate concern—and you've really laid it on the line. Your life is now about this, whatever it is. He says there's always going to be the nagging doubt: "What if I am fooling myself? What if this really is *not* the ultimate thing—this religion? This revolution? Suppose I am wasting my life?" Well, you cannot just sit on the fence. You've got to live your life for *some*thing—okay, I am going to take that risk and there's always the risk of faith because of existential doubt. Is it really worthwhile?

But right in the middle there is *methodological* doubt that is at the heart of science and history and all sorts of inquiries like that where it's built into the method, where you have to scrutinize all the evidence. You say, "I am looking for a conclusion; I seek to verify a hypothesis, but the way to do it is to see if it can be falsified." Can it stand the test? What hurdles can I erect for it to jump over—because it's going to have to do that. It's got to pass the test. So what test can I devise? You've got to be skeptical about it.

He says if someone is committed to the inquiry coming out a particular way—the facts being this way and not that way—hoping and betting that when the day is done Jesus will have proven to have risen from the dead or the exodus will be vindicated as a real historical event; knowing that tomorrow some new evidence might come up. I am reading a bunch of novels right now about lost gospel discoveries. There are about 45 of these things that I have been able to come up with and I am writing a book on them. In them someone comes up with some new Dead Sea scroll or some new Nag Hammadi text written by Jesus or by Joseph of Arimathea explaining where he put the body of Jesus, and there was no resurrection. Fascinating stuff! This could happen. We are finding surprising discoveries of manuscripts and it could happen—all it would take is some sort of authentic Roman register of crucified prisoners, one of them Jesus the Nazarene, a historical Jesus would be secured. Or a letter from somebody saying, "I heard this Jesus preach in a synagogue, he's not bad." We have stuff like that about Apollonius of Tyana, for instance. Nobody is trying to prove anything, they just happen to mention that they saw the great man. That would anchor the character as a historical figure. Alas, no such thing is present in the case of Jesus, whether it's bad luck or because there was no Jesus, who knows? But some such discovery might be made, and faith would hinge on that.

Or the opposite might happen, something that would debunk a historical Jesus. But the believer says, because of what he's got invested, "I am just betting that won't happen. I am just betting that any fair analysis of the facts is going to come out my way." And of course then you get into a bind—and Van Harvey talks about this in his great book *The Historian and the Believer*—you can never know if your judgments are being made with a good conscience anymore, because you might be subconsciously warping your judgment of the evidence because of what you would *like* to believe to be true. (Of course, the same danger would exist in the case of a polemicist who was dead set on proving Jesus was no more than a myth.) Tillich says this is the kind of mess you get into if you are rooting for some particular result. If your ultimate concern depends upon a dubious historical proposition, a theory, a reconstruction that might wind up being true, or it might not, or you might never know, what business do you have saying, "Yeah, it's *got* to be true, so I *believe* it to be true"?

That's just producing a fault line that is going to commit you to dishonesty in your historical work—and every book of apologetics shows that. Tillich says, "Fundamentalism has demonic aspects in that it splits the conscience of its thoughtful adherents and forces them to suppress aspects of the truth of which they are dimly aware." So why is the fundamentalist apologist on the warpath? "We have met the enemy, and he is us!" The unbeliever against whom he goes into battle is in his own mind. You're just ruining your faith by infecting it with a doubt you could never get rid of, and you're just ruining your historical study by confusing what belief is. Is it an ultimate concern or is it a dubious opinion that you must persuade yourself is *not* dubious?

What about doubt as part of historical method? I just want to explain how that is so—and how this is not tailored specifically to deal with claims that supernatural events have happened, rather just how the whole idea of historical method has to do with skepticism. I think of a great, great book—really a transcription of lectures—*The Idea of History* by R.G. Collingwood, an English historian who thought like a German one. His book overlapped a great deal with F. H. Bradley's *The Presuppositions of Critical History*. Bradley was explaining and defending the Tübingen School: F.C. Baur, D.F. Strauss, et. al., their work and its presuppositions. Collingwood goes into the history of history writing, the history of historiography, and he says modern history writing is a very different thing from what the so-called historians of the ancient world did. Another great work in the same vein is by Bernard Lewis, *History: Remembered, Recovered, Invented*, in which he shows that virtually all ancient so-called history was legitimization narrative. It was all trying to explain how things got the way they are now with the divinely ordained regime of Julius Caesar or whomever—and of course that's obviously the case, obvious to us, with the Bible.

Well, Collingwood said sometimes there were people in the Middle Ages who tried to improve things a bit. They didn't have any real axe to grind and did legitimately wonder what had happened in the past. What did they do? They were "scissors and paste" historians, as he called them. They regarded the documents from the past as "authorities." The historian must deal with his "authorities." In fact you still see this in footnotes in the Revised Standard Version, when it says "some authorities have this reading"—they mean "some of our manuscripts have this reading;" and, yeah, they used to call all the historical sources our "authorities." So they tell us all we're ever going to know, and it's our job to try to reconcile them if they appear to contradict one another, to re-read them and see how we can work that out because we're really at their mercy. We don't know any better, we can't get into a time machine. All we've got to go on is what the ancients have bequeathed us, and so let's see if we can just preserve as much of that as we can and iron it out. Well, that's pre-critical history writing.

Modern critical history began when historians realized the documents—the reports of the past—are not *authorities*, they are *sources*. It is the *historian* who is the authority. Maybe he doesn't want to be; but you've got to pick and choose. You've got to call them like you see them, because those contradictions—I'm talking about Pliny, the Bible, the *Gallic Wars*, whatever—those contradictions within and between sources show you that you can't just read it off the page as if it all happened, and you do have to take into account the axe-grinding character of it, and you find anachronisms and various other signs that all is not well with these as factual reports. So you must become the authority to adjudicate, however tentatively, what you think really did happen behind the documents. Sometimes it's helpful information, but sometimes the evidence is not evidence for what it pretends to be evidence for! Sorry for that sentence, but, he says, there is a history of propaganda.

For instance, in my New Testament dissertation *The Widow Traditions in Luke-Acts* I try to show how all the material about women in those two New Testament books do not just describe the state of women in the early church but are trying to put down the role of women and restrict it. And so you're not reading the way it really *was* but the way someone thought it *should* have been—not *description* but *prescription*. You have to learn how to interpret the evidence, and it is not simply a matter of believing it or accepting it. That's over-simplistic. And again this does not necessarily get into claims of the supernatural. It might, but it follows through with all history writing.

And how does the historian proceed? It's the old "hermeneutical circle" Heidegger and others talked about. You begin with a hypothesis—a hypothetical understanding in broad terms—of what your study has led you to believe the past was like—admittedly open to correction, and that is what you hope you're going to do. You look at the various documents and evidence in light of that and begin to revise your initial hypothesis. It's admittedly circular but in a corrective way—back to the drawing board, that kind of way—and yet the further you refine it the more sharp the lens is through which you now view the evidence, and you begin to develop criteria—"Yeah, it *says* this… but it couldn't have happened because of this and that."

That tells us two more things that Ernst Troeltsch, German theologian and historian, expounded very effectively. Okay, the historian is the authority, the documents are the sources, now what sort of judgments can we make, and how are they made? Well, this idea that you approach it with an initial understanding of the past, always hoping to correct it—how else could you describe that understanding of the past? Troeltsch said it would be good to speak of it as—he wasn't directly referring to Collingwood, I am just saying the ideas sort of bounce off each other this way—you would use the *principle of analogy*, among others. You would say if I do not bring to historical reports the working hypothesis that things have always happened more or less the way we see them happen now, no judgment of probability is possible.

Suppose somebody says, "Gee, in this story it says that so and so changed into a werewolf on April 15th. Then I guess it's true!" No. You don't want to have to be at the mercy of any old legend. Some medieval chronicler, for example, says, "Oh, you know, it rained blood out of the sky today; it literally rained cats and dogs; or a ship flew through the air and dropped anchor and somebody climbed down the anchor rope and then left to get a pizza" or whatever. Well, do you have to believe these things because your "authorities," the documents, say so? No, you doubt it. It looks odd because you know things like this do not happen—or if they do, somebody's been keeping them a secret pretty well. This just is not the kind of thing that ever happens! I know somebody will pop up and say, "You're a uniformitarian! You believe dogmatically things must have always happened the way they do now!" Well, do *you* believe it used to rain literal cats and dogs? Is there really any chance of that? Why doesn't it anymore? Why did it change? Maybe it did. But the thing is, we're just up the creek at the mercy of any crazy assertion if you don't have some criterion of probability, and the only one you've got, for better or worse, is present-day experience.

That gives you only the right to rule on what *probably* happened—

or probably *didn't* happen, and that's Troeltsch's other big principle that I want to mention: the inevitable *tentativeness*, the *provisionality* of all historical reconstructions. No real historian will tell you that the resurrection of Jesus is the best attested fact in history, as several people say, and therefore we have to accept it. Gary Habermas, another friend of mine (I hate to quote him like this), says if an assertion is accepted by a whole lot of people for a long time we can consider it a fact. No we can't. I'm afraid we can't do that. So we decide what the facts are. We have to decide which ones *are* facts. What do we *mean* by "facts," and so forth. And the best you can do is to make a tentative judgment. You can't just have a majority vote on what people think, see what a historical pedigree an idea had, see how long someone believed it. I guess more people probably believed the earth was flat than now believe that it isn't. But it isn't flat, sorry about that.

But the historian has to say, "Here's the way it looks at present." But, yeah, it's open to change—and of course that's the scientific approach, too. That's the whole paradigm succession thing that Thomas S. Kuhn (*The Structure of Scientific Revolutions*) talks about: you want to come up with the best tentative model you can, and if somebody else shoots it down—great! All we want is to get closer to the truth, which we're never quite going to get to, probably because it's kind of a North Star by which we navigate. You're never going to get on board your boat and get to the North Star. No, it's like a guiding light; you're trying to get closer and closer to it—you're trying to get farther and farther out of your ignorance. But who knows? It's conceivable somebody might come up with some alternative paradigm to evolution. But if they did, it would have to explain all the evidence as well or better. It's kind of doubtful anybody will, it will be a heck of a boulder to try to push, to accomplish such a thing, so I don't expect it will happen, but nobody would rule it out because all results of honest inquiry are based on this skepticism and contain the seed of their own demolition. It may never happen, but you're willing to consider any view.

All historical judgments pretend to be no more than provisional, and you can see the problem right here when somebody claims to be a historian but is arguing for a favorite belief—like N. T. Wright. He's a used car salesman; he's like Jerry Falwell in a better suit. N. T. Wright and all these guys posing as historians making historical judgments—you're just being conned! They don't understand what history writing is, just like a Creationist does not understand what science is. It's not that they're just doing a bad job of it. It's not that they're just cheating like the guys at Duke with the Rhine Institute, pulling the plug to get the machines to read the right way and giving you evidence, like the Ghost Busters, for ESP. No, they just don't know what science is. And that's the problem with Christian believers trying to back up their beliefs and prove them with historical evidence. You can't arrive at anything more than a provisional judgment. You just cannot establish belief by history; that's not what historians do.

My favorite example of the principle of analogy is this. Suppose you come back home from a long day's work, you just plop down on a chair, and click on the TV with your remote. You don't notice what channel it is. You weren't the last one to use it. The first thing you see on the screen is a giant reptile looming above the Tokyo skyline stomping the buildings into matchsticks. What's your first reaction? "Oh! CNN!" No, you realize, "Oh, I got the SyFy channel," *Godzilla*, *The Lost World*, something like that. Well, you don't *know* that. There you go with those presuppositions again, your anti-monster dogmatic worldview. I mean, it's conceivable. I can imagine Gojira coming up out of the water and all that. I don't know how it could be. I can't rule it out, but I can't take it too seriously either because, though I know of no such experience reported by any reliable (or *un*reliable) witness, I *do* know of plenty of cheesy Toho Studio flicks in which this happens, and so I have to assume this is another one. I could be wrong. It's a probabilistic judgment, but what are the chances? And that's all you've got.

So the one who is skeptical of the resurrection of Jesus, the Red Sea thing, a talking donkey—it's not that the historian says, "I *know* this never happened because it *couldn't* have happened." No historian has any business saying that. All you can say is that there's just no reason to say that it's probable. If we could get back into a time machine, who knows what the results would be? I won't lay the odds down. But since we can't, we have to judge it as "improbable." And that's not good enough for religious believers and apologists, and they say, "Well, suppose it *did* happen. You're just cutting yourself off from knowing about it." Okay, I guess I am. But that's just the way it is with history. We're not pretending to have some sort of reverse clairvoyance where, by faith, we can see the past, like Rudolf Steiner thought he could; you know, Madame Blavatsky and others thought they could just imagine the past, and they were seeing it, and that's what happened—Atlantis, Lemuria, all that stuff.

So I ask the so-called historian—the apologist—what other access do you think *you* have? It's inevitably probabilistic like Karl Barth and other theologians with orthodox beliefs freely admitted. Raymond E. Brown, for instance, a great Roman Catholic critical New Testament scholar—here's a guy that said, in effect, "I don't see any real evidence for the virgin birth of Jesus, though I do believe it as a Roman Catholic, but I don't believe it as a historian. I wouldn't try to establish it." It's like he's claiming an alternate epistemology; it boils down to *the will to believe*: "I was told this happened, I want to believe it, and that's how I know it's true." But you *don't* know it's true. And I don't know that it's false, but all I'm claiming is, it seems improbable because that's all any historical judgment is.

So that's how skepticism is built right into scientific and historical method. It's not a tool used by skeptics or unbelievers to gain their ends, as believers would have you think. No, that's just what the method is. And if we don't have it we're just stuck with sheer credulity.

The Synoptic Apocalypse
and the Son of Man

One goal of this article is to demonstrate that, as Stanley Fish[1] suggests, what we deem the "natural" or "literal" or "plain" sense of the text is often simply the accustomed reading, the one that strikes us as self-evident just because everyone in our interpretive community takes it for granted.[2] A new (to us) reading seems implausible only because it is unfamiliar to us. The other main objective is to challenge an objection frequently lodged against the Unificationist teaching that the Lord of the Second Advent need not be Jesus Christ himself. The two turn out to be one and the same, since the conventional belief that the gospels depict Jesus predicting his own personal apocalyptic reappearance may be gratuitous. This is going to entail a rather lengthy running start. Everything hinges on the denotation of the notoriously perplexing phrase "the son of man," especially as it occurs in certain apocalyptic gospel passages. And preparatory to this, it will be necessary to isolate these passages from others in which "son of man" has very different implications. By ignoring these differences, many[3] have blurred the gospels' eschatological teaching. When the proper distinctions are restored, the apocalyptic picture vis-à-vis Jesus may look quite different.

---

1 Stanley Fish, *Is There a Text in this Class? The Authority of Interpretive Communities* (Cambridge: Harvard University Press, 1980), pp. 276-277.

2 Peter L. Berger and Thomas Luckmann, *The Social Construction of Reality: A Treatise in the Sociology of Knowledge* (Garden City: Doubleday Anchor Books, 1967), p. 87.

3 E.g., George Eldon Ladd, *The Presence of the Future: The Eschatology of Biblical Realism* (Grand Rapids: Eerdmans, 1974), pp. 214, 324-325.

EVERY MOTHER'S SON (OF MAN)

As Geza Vermes[1] has explained, a frequent use of the Aramaic *bar nasha* ("son of man") was to refer to the perennial conditions, duties, vicissitudes, and prerogatives of mankind in general, often invoked on one's own behalf. We still speak in this way, as when one says, "You really know how to hurt a guy!" In other words, "You really hurt *me*." In the film *The Whole Wide World*, a frustrated Robert E. Howard, white knuckles gripping his steering wheel, tells his girlfriend, "A man's got to have a purpose!" Of course he means that *he* is struggling to find his purpose. He possesses the needs and the rights of all men.

Once I saw an episode of the old *Donahue* talk show. Phil was interrogating a Hasidic Jew about his tradition's less familiar customs. He asked if it was actually true that Hasid husband and wife have intercourse naked but, for modesty's sake, only through a hole in a sheet placed between them. The gentleman, obviously very ill at ease, replied, "It is an outrage to mankind!" Phil seemed completely clueless, apparently thinking the man meant it was an anti-Semitic slur, but I recognized his meaning: "How dare you? You are embarrassing me!" Such a question must scandalize the son of man.

The Hadith of Muhammad show the currency of the idiom in Arabic, too: "The son of Man has no more right than that he should have a house wherein he may live, and a piece of cloth whereby he may hide his nakedness, and a chip of bread, and water."[2] The sentiment is the same as that expressed in 1 Timothy 6:6-8: "There is great gain in godliness with contentment; for we brought nothing into the world, and we cannot take anything out of the world; but if we have food and clothing, with these we shall be content." "The son of Man" in the Hadith equals "we" in 1 Timothy, and that is the logic of the idiom.

An outstanding example from the gospels shows Jesus defending his forgiving the sins of a paralytic. His critics are affronted: surely only

---

1 Geza Vermes, *Jesus the Jew: A Historian's Reading of the Gospels* (London: Fontana/Collins, 1976), pp. 180-182.

2 Mirza Abul-Fazl, ed. and trans., *Sayings of the Prophet Muhammad* (New Delhi: Award Publishing Company, 1980), p. 35.

God has the power (the right) to forgive sinners! Jesus then performs an act that he offers as proof, not that he uniquely shares the prerogatives of deity, pulling rank, but rather that God has placed forgiveness of sins within the human purview. Mark 2:10; Matthew 9:6; Luke 5:24: "'But that you may know that the son of man[1] has authority on earth to forgive sins'—he said to the paralytic—'Rise, take up your bed and go home.'" Matthew certainly understood the story as vindicating the notion that human beings, not just Jesus, can forgive sins: the witnesses "glorified God, who had given such authority to *men*," not exclusively to Jesus. In view is a division of labor, as in Psalm 115:16; "The heavens are the LORD's heavens, but the earth he has given to the sons of men." Just so, God forgives from heaven, but he has authorized his people to pronounce forgiveness here on earth. Also see Matthew 16:19.

Likewise in Mark 2:28; Matthew 12:8; Luke 6:5: "The son of man is lord even of the sabbath." Again, Jesus is not spilling the beans about his supposed Messiahship, so carefully guarded throughout Mark's gospel, but rather affirming the right of human beings since, after all, God created the Sabbath as a gift to a weary humanity, not a legalistic burden as if God first ordained the Sabbath, then realized he was going to need some people to observe it. It is humanity who is Lord of the Sabbath, not the other way around.

Bible readers have long puzzled over the seeming subordinationist Christology (cf. John 14:28; 1 Cor. 11:3) of Matthew 12:32, "Whoever says a word against the son of man will be forgiven; but whoever speaks against the Holy Spirit will not be forgiven, either in this age or in the age to come" (cf. Luke 12:10). Now why should badmouthing the Messiah or Jesus (if that is what "son of man" means here) be deemed a less serious infraction than trash-talking the Holy Ghost? Something is wrong here, namely that the intended denotation of "son of man" is once again "human beings, mortals," not the Second

---

1 I capitalize "Son of Man" when I believe the phrase refers to the apocalyptic deliverer or the Christian savior. By contrast, I do not capitalize it when I think the reference is to mankind in general, invoked on the speaker's behalf or apotropaically.

Person of the Trinity or the Messiah. And "the Holy Spirit" denotes simply "God." You see, given the context, where the subject is avoiding inappropriate speech about God, the saying is taking special care not, so to speak, to take the name of "God" in vain. The idea is to "hallow thy name" via pious circumlocution: "the Holy Spirit," not just "God." We see the same thing, for instance, in Jesus' exchange with the Sanhedrin: "Are you the Christ, the Son of the *Blessed One*?" "You shall see the Son of Man sitting at the right hand of *Power*." The issue in Matthew 12:32/Luke12:10 is not to contrast Jesus blasphemy versus Holy Spirit blasphemy. Rather, it is blasphemy (e.g., slander) against fellow mortals versus cursing God. The latter is unforgivable because (ala Anselm) it offends the infinite honor of God, requiring infinite retribution.

This interpretation is secured by comparison with Mark 3:28-29: "Truly, I say to you, all sins will be forgiven the sons of men, and whatever blasphemies they utter; but whoever blasphemes the Holy Spirit never has forgiveness, but is guilty of an eternal sin." This is a more primitive version of the same saying, and here it is clear that the reference is to the sons of men, not to a Messianic figure.

Mark 14:21/Matt 26:24/Luke 22:22 ("For the son of man goes as it is written of him, but woe to that man by whom the son of man is betrayed! It would have been better for that man if he had not been born."), according to the present narrative context, is obviously an attempt to answer the early Christian question: was Judas Iscariot a villain deserving the worst possible damnation, or was he a necessary component in the foreordained plan of salvation and thus a kind of high priest offering up the sacrifice of Christ?

But originally it was not so. We find an earlier version of the saying in Matthew 18:6-7: " but whoever causes one of these little ones who believe in me to sin, it would be better for him to have a great millstone fastened round his neck and to be drowned in the depth of the sea. Woe to the world for temptations to sin! For it is necessary that temptations come, but woe to the man by whom the temptation comes!" This version has nothing to do with the prophesied betrayal of Jesus but rather with the inevitability of temptations and trials all human beings must endure. But if you are the occasion for another's misfortune or temptation, the fact that, if *you* weren't the stumbling block someone else *would* be, does not excuse you. Whoever is to blame will wish he could be retroactively erased from existence.

The saying in Matthew 8:20/Luke 9:58, "Foxes have holes, and birds of the air have nests; but the son of man has nowhere to lay his head," has been quite plausibly explained as a kind of recruitment slogan used by the charismatic itinerants, warning potential recruits about what they must give up once they join the wandering brethren. And indeed it may well have so functioned, but that was not its origin. At first, the son of man denoted "mankind," and the point was apparently that humans have no one natural habitat, unlike other species. Or perhaps it described the self-understanding of nomadic tribes. A suggestive parallel is found in Plutarch's *Life of Tiberius Gracchus*.

> The beasts of the field and the birds of the air have their holes and hiding places, but the men who fight and die for Italy enjoy only the light and the air. Our generals urge their soldiers to fight for the graves and shrines of their ancestors. The appeal is idle and false, you cannot point to a paternal altar. You have no ancestral tomb. You fight and die to give wealth and luxury to others. You are called the masters of the world, but you do not have a foot of ground that you can call your own.[1]

"The son of man came eating and drinking, and they say, 'Behold, a glutton and a drunkard, a friend of tax collectors and sinners!'" (Matt.11:19; Luke 7:34). Who? Originally not necessarily Jesus. It is certainly typical of the kind of vilification aimed at "backsliders" and "compromisers" by blue-nosed religious ascetics like the Qumran monks. If sectarian rivals observed different regulations governing marital intercourse, they blasted them as "fornicators" and "sinners." Such vehement polemic probably was an extreme form of "building a hedge around the Torah": don't give sensual pleasure an inch or it will take a mile. So once again, "son of man" means "everyman."

As if we required more proof that the gospel writers understood

---

1 Quoted in Gary Courtney, *Et tu, Judas? Then Fall Jesus!* (Lincoln NE: iUniverse, 1992, 2004), p. 140.

that sometimes "son of man" was a simple self-reference rather than a Messianic title, compare Matthew 16:13 ("he asked his disciples, 'Who do men say that the son of man is?'") with the earlier version Mark 8:27 ("Who do men say that I am?"). Matthew has not inserted a Christological title. If that was his intent, he bungled it, since he would have pre-empted the disciples' reply by giving them the right answer right there in the question! And they *still* get it wrong! No, Rabbi Matthew knew better than that.

Another: Luke 6:22 has "Blessed are you when men hate you, and when they exclude you and revile you, and cast out your name as evil, on account of the son of man!" But Matthew 5:11 alters this to "Blessed are you when men revile you and persecute you and utter all kinds of evil against you falsely on *my* account"—with no change in meaning.

Luke 22:48 has Jesus say to his betrayer, "Judas, would you betray the son of man with a kiss?" I take this as a bitter and ironic rebuke of Judas' hypocrisy: "Really? You betray a guy with a *kiss*? Drop the pretense; you've exposed your true colors!"

YOU KNOW WHO

A related use of "son of man" is what we might call "ominous self-reference,"[1] where one fears to invoke misfortune by speaking of the possibility in connection with oneself. "Speak of the devil and he'll appear." "Keep your head down!" Jesus is often depicted speaking thusly of himself. There is no thought here of the prophesied Messiah, but only of averting bad luck. It is also an expression of modesty, declining praise, lest one poach upon the glory due to God alone. Pride goeth before a fall. Even Jesus must defer to God's glory: "Why do you call *me* good? No one is good but God alone" (Mark 10:18). Too bad Herod Agrippa didn't have the same modest reserve (Acts 12:21-23).

When Jesus speaks of the coming arrest and execution of the "son of man" (Matt. 17:12, 22; 20:18; 26:2; Mark 8:31; 9:12; 10:33; 14:41; Luke 9:22, 44; John 8:28), he is merely employing this once-familiar idiom. Even John 13:31 ("When [Judas] had gone out, Jesus said,

---

1 Vermes, *Jesus the Jew*, p. 168.

'Now is the son of man glorified, and in him God is glorified.'") fits the pattern since John speaks of Jesus' elevation on the cross as the moment of his glorification.

Christian theologians love to cite these sayings to support the "radical" or "dialectical" Christology according to which the heavenly Son of Man shows his glory in his suffering on the cross. But, even though such a piece of theology, albeit in other vocabulary, does occur in the New Testament (1 Cor. 1:18), there is nothing of it in these son man logia which simply have Jesus speaking of the fact of coming misfortune.

ONE LIKE A SON OF MAN

Maurice Casey shows that Daniel's vision of the celestial "one like a son of man" did not mean to establish "son of man" as a Messianic title, role, or figure. Nor do we find it so used in subsequent centuries of Jewish literature. Careful analysis led Casey to conclude that apocalyptic references to the Son of Man seem to function as a shorthand allusion to the Daniel 7 scenario, signaling the eschatological deliverance of righteous Israel.[1] Norman Perrin suggests that Son of Man had not become a Messianic title even in the *New* Testament. Again, the gospel apocalyptic passages in which the Son of Man is mentioned look like patchwork peshers, i.e., artificial stitching together of out-of-context verses, a common, if fanciful, exegetical technique ubiquitous in Judaism from the Dead Sea Scrolls on up through the Kabbalah.[2]

But even if we think "Son of Man" *is* supposed to be a title for an End Time deliverer in the gospel apocalyptic verses, it is only the evangelists/redactors who identified the apocalyptic Son of Man with Jesus.[3] The texts themselves, attributed to Jesus in the larger narrative

---

1 Maurice Casey, *The Son of Man: The Interpretation and Influence of Daniel 7* (London: SPCK, 1979).

2 Norman Perrin, *A Modern Pilgrimage in New Testament Christology* (Philadelphia: Fortress Press, 1974), Chapter III, "The Son of Man in Ancient Judaism and Primitive Christianity," pp. 23-40.

3 Rudolf Bultmann, *The History of the Synoptic Tradition*. Trans. John Marsh

context, refer to the Son of Man in the third person, not the first. The Son of Man is *he*, not *I*. The sayings, in their original isolation, gave no name to the Son Man. Indeed, looking at these sayings one by one, it seems obvious that they are not quotes from a prophet about his own glorious destiny but rather little more than redundant paraphrases of the Son of Man passage in Daniel chapter 7.

> I saw in the night visions, and behold, with the clouds of heaven there came one like a son of man, and he came to the Ancient of Days and was presented before him. (Dan. 7:13)

Matthew 16:27-28: "For the Son of Man is to come with his angels in the glory of his Father, and then *he* will repay every man for what he has done. Truly, I say to you, there are some standing here who will not taste death before they see the Son of man coming in *his* kingdom."

Mark 13:26: "And then they will see the Son of Man coming in clouds with great power and glory."

In Mark 8:38 Jesus warns that "whoever is ashamed of me and of my words in this adulterous and sinful generation, of him will the Son of Man also be ashamed, when *he* comes in the glory of *his* Father with the holy angels."[1] For one thing, as Gerd Theissen notes, the distinction drawn between "me" and "he" in this saying reflects the ministry of the itinerant charismatics who saw themselves as the earthly mouthpieces of their heavenly patron the Son of Man on the one hand, and, and on the other, that Son of Man who will vindicate them upon his soon appearing. But the Son of Man is not yet identified as Jesus. In Matthew 10:32-33 this has changed. The saying has been Christianized. Matthew has Jesus speaking of himself *as* the Son of Man: "So every one who acknowledges *me* before men, I also will acknowledge before my Father who is in heaven; but whoever denies *me* before men, I also will deny before my Father who is in heaven."

In Mark 14:62 Jesus tells his judges that their roles will someday be

---

(New York: Harper & Row, 1968), pp. 121, 122.

1 Gerd Theissen, *Sociology of Early Palestinian Christianity.* Trans. John Bowden (Philadelphia: Fortress Press, 1978), p. 27.

reversed, but, again, the context in which the Son of Man saying has been embedded is secondary. On its own, we find an independent prediction that the speaker's contemporaries will live to see the fulfillment of Daniel's prophetic vision: "You will see the Son of Man seated at the right hand of Power, and coming with the clouds of heaven." Ditto Matthew 26:64: "I tell you, hereafter you will see the Son of Man seated at the right hand of Power, and coming on the clouds of heaven." (Luke 22:68-69, "But from now on the Son of man shall be seated at the right hand of the power of God," removes, characteristic of him, the element of Jesus' own generation still being alive at the time of the Parousia.)

Matthew 19:28: "Truly, I say to you, in the new world, when the Son of Man shall sit on his glorious throne, you who have followed me will also sit on twelve thrones, judging the twelve tribes of Israel."

Matthew 24:27: "For as the lightning comes from the east and shines as far as the west, so will be the coming of the Son of Man."

Luke 17:24: "For as the lightning flashes and lights up the sky from one side to the other, so will the Son of Man be in his day."

Matthew 24:30: "Then will appear the sign of the Son of Man in heaven, and then all the tribes of the earth will mourn, and they will see the Son of Man coming on the clouds of heaven with power and great glory."

Matthew 24:39: "They did not know until the flood came and swept them all away, so will be the coming of the Son of Man."

Matthew 24:44: "Therefore you also must be ready; for the Son of Man is coming at an hour you do not expect."

Matthew 25:31: "When the Son of Man comes in his glory, and all the angels with him, then he will sit on his glorious throne."

Luke 17:22: "The days are coming when you will desire to see one of the days of the Son of Man, and you will not see it."[1]

Luke 17:26: "As it was in the days of Noah, so will it be in the days of the Son of Man."

Luke 17:30: "So will it be on the day when the Son of Man is revealed."

---

1 Here again we see Luke's redactional theme of the delay of the Parousia.

Luke 18:8: "I tell you, he will vindicate them speedily. Neverthe-less, when the Son of Man comes, will he find faith on earth?"

Luke 21:27: "And then they will see the Son of Man coming in a cloud with power and great glory."

Luke 21:36: "But watch at all times, praying that you may have strength to escape all these things that will take place, and to stand before the Son of Man."

John 1:51: "Truly, truly, I say to you, you will see heaven opened, and the angels of God ascending and descending upon the Son of Man."

"He has given him authority to execute judgment, because he is the Son of Man" (John 5:27), like the next two Johannine texts, seems to reflect passages from 1 Enoch, as Edgar J. Goodspeed once observed.[1] This is especially interesting since the Book of Enoch is heavily depen-dent upon Daniel chapter 7's vision of the Son of Man who takes the heavenly throne at the right hand of the Ancient of Days. Debate con-tinues over the identity of Daniel's "one like a son of man coming with the clouds of heaven," but it is perfectly clear that "that Son of man" in the Book of Enoch is the eponymous patriarch whose righteous life earned him an ascension to heaven. There he was transfigured into superhuman form and was invested as the Son of Man. His forgot-ten identity with the heavenly Enoch (or Metatron)[2] was revealed to him, and he was sent back to earth to vouchsafe his newly learned se-crets to his family before returning to heaven. These revelations form the contents of 1 Enoch (and several other Enochian scriptures). John 5:27 seems to refer to the investiture of the ascended Enoch once he is revealed as the Son of Man. Once Christians decided that Jesus, not Enoch, was the pre-existent Son of Man from Daniel, the whole story was applied to him. John's gospel takes this for granted.

Similarly, John 6:62 ("What if you were to see the Son of Man as-cending where he was before?") sounds awfully like Enoch, antici-

---

1 J. Goodspeed somewhere noted the phrase as a virtually verbatim quota-tion of 1 Enoch LXIX: "The sum of judgment was given to the Son of Man."

2 Andrei A. Orlov, *The Enoch-Metatron Tradition*. Texts and Studies in An-cient Judaism 107 (Tubingen: Mohr Siebeck, 2005).

pating his second departure from earth to heaven, his teaching completed. In its present, Johannine, context, this saying seems like Jesus' rebuke to disciples confused by their teacher's claim that he has come down from heaven. They of course didn't and couldn't have witnessed Jesus' descent from heaven, since it happened via an at least apparently human birth with nothing outwardly to mark it as divine (John 7:28). But if the doubters were actually to witness Jesus' ascension into the sky? Would that finally convince them?[1] One wonders if perhaps in some underlying version of an Enochian text, this saying was a challenge to Enoch's relatives who knew only that old Enoch had gone missing, soon returning to impart tall tales of a heavenly journey, and wondered if the old man was just spinning yarns.

John 3:13 ("No one has ascended into heaven but he who descended from heaven, the Son of Man") makes more sense in an Enochian context, since Enoch was believed to have ascended (to say nothing of Elijah) many centuries before Jesus who therefore, even as a purely literary character, can hardly have denied the famous ascension recounted in scripture, which is what the traditional reading implies.

John 6:27 says, "Do not labor for the food which perishes, but for the food which endures to eternal life, which the Son of Man will give to you; for on him has God the Father set his seal." In its present Johannine setting, the sentence seems to refer to Jesus' provision of sacramental bread in the present (or in the immediate future), bread that will guarantee eternal life. But with Enoch as the Son of Man, the reference would be to the extravagant Millennial bounty .

SON OF MAN CHRISTOLOGY

We have seen that, in some otherwise parallel apocalyptic sayings, one uses "the Son of Man," while the other has replaced that phrase with

---

1 Maybe not; keep in mind that Jesus' "glorification" occurred on the cross, perhaps implying that the "ascension" appeared no more overtly miraculous than the "descent," that, just as the "descent" looked outwardly no different from a normal human birth, the "ascension" appeared to be simply another human death.

"I" or other explicit self-reference. These changes seem to attest a process of adjustment, making a connection originally absent, identifying the unnamed Danielic Son of Man with the Christian founder. In the next handful of verses this process has advanced farther. In them "Son of Man" has simply become synonymous with Jesus, as per Christian Christology ever since.

Matt 12:40: "For as Jonah was three days and three nights in the belly of the whale, so will the Son of Man be three days and three nights in the heart of the earth." This one is a purely redactional creation by the Matthean evangelist, who hereby hammers in a nail from which he will hang the subsequent episode in which the Sanhedrinists approach Pilate to warn him of an anticipated resurrection hoax. "We remember how that imposter said, while he was still alive, 'After three days I will rise again'" (Matt. 27:63). How did they know this? Because, only in this gospel, Jesus publicly promises he will be resurrected. Pretty convenient.

Luke 19:10: "For the Son of Man came to seek and to save the lost." Bultmann[1] pointed out that all such statements beginning with "The Son of Man came to…" or "I came to…" betray by their retrospective tone their secondary character. They are someone's retrospective summations of the saving mission of Jesus. The unification of "Jesus" and "the Son of Man" is taken for granted here.

Mark 10:45/Matt. 20:28, "For the Son of Man also came not to be served but to serve, and to give his life as a ransom for many," is another instance of the same trend. In addition, it seems plausible that an earlier or original version might be preserved in Luke 22:27, "For which is the greater, one who sits at table, or one who serves? Is it not the one who sits at table? But I am among you as one who serves." Not only not apocalyptic, but not even a son of man saying. (Of course, it is also possible that Luke omitted the son of man reference along with the ransom business.)[2]

John 6:53, "Truly, truly, I say to you, unless you eat the flesh of the

---

1 Bultmann, *History of the Synoptic Tradition*, p. 155.

2 Why would Luke omit the ransom element? No doubt because the ransom idea was too Marcionite for his taste.

Son of Man and drink his blood, you have no life in you," dates from long after the mutation of Jesus into the Son of Man (and vice versa), attesting the assimilation of Christianity to its fellow Mystery cults where initiates ate bread and drank wine (or beer) as the body and blood of Osiris and Dionysus.

What about John 9:35? "Jesus heard that they had cast him out, and having found him he said, 'Do you believe in the Son of Man?'" This has to be an invitation *to the reader*, for whom the blind man stands. (Especially since the premise of the scene is a gross anachronism, retrojecting the expulsion of Jesus-believers from the synagogues, which this very gospel elsewhere (16:4) places in the future vis-à-vis Jesus and the disciples.) Even so, "son of man" still might be a self-reference, "Do you believe in me?" except for the fact that the blind man understands Jesus to be referring to someone else: "Who is he, sir, that I may believe in him?"

We have seen that, while the gospels ascribe numerous "son of man" sayings to Jesus, none of them have Jesus assign himself a role in the apocalyptic denouement. Several sayings predict the End Time events, but the agent of salvation and judgment bears no personal name (certainly not that of Jesus) but is referred to as the (Danielic-Enochian) "Son of Man." But what about Mark 13:5-6? "Take heed that no one leads you astray. Many will come in my name, saying, 'I am he!' and they will lead many astray." Do we not here find Jesus warning that imposters will one day seek to co-opt his great name and messianic role for their own nefarious purposes? So must we not have here the missing puzzle piece: Jesus laying claim to the messianic mantle? Are not centuries of Bible readers, then, justified in inferring that the Son of Man in Mark 13 is supposed to be Jesus himself?

At this point I want to propose a new possibility for understanding Mark 13:5-6, as stemming originally from a *non-Christian* sectarian source. What if we are to understand the lying claims of the pseudo-prophets as *Christian* claims that *Jesus* is the Son of Man, that it is *he* whose Parousia believers must expect. But if this is the intent of the text, what on earth is it doing in the obviously Christian Gospel of Mark?

Actually, that would not be all that extraordinary given the context of ancient sectarian competitiveness. Bultmann[1] argued (quite compellingly to me) that the Logos Hymn, now part of the Johannine Prologue, was originally a piece of liturgy used in the Gnostic-Mandaean sect of John the Baptist, brought over to the Jesus sect, with names appropriately switched, by a convert to the rival Jesus sect. Likewise, it looks quite probable that the nativity material about the Baptist in Luke 1:5-25, 57-80 derived from the hagiographic lore of the/a Baptist sect, especially in view of verses 68-69 which seem to make John the Davidic Messiah. The saying "Among those born of women, none is greater than John" (Matt. 11:11a/Luke 7:28) reads like John the Baptist Christology, receiving Christian "correction" (co-optation) in the second half of the verse. Matthew 11:12-13/Luke 16:16 looks like a claim that the Baptizer, not Jesus, was the object of scriptural prophecy. The dialogue with the Samaritan woman in John chapter 4 looks suspiciously like a vestige of the succession dispute between the two Gnostic/Messianic sects of Dositheus[2] and Simon Magus, both split-offs from the Baptist's sect. Verse 10, "If you knew the gift of God and who it is that is [speaking] to you," etc. Who was originally the thirsty speaker? Dositheus, whose name means "gift of God." And the identity of the Samaritan woman? She must have been Helen, consort of Simon Magus, who rescued her from prostitution, here represented by the five husbands plus one paramour. And let's not forget Paul's eyebrow-raising mention (2 Cor. 11:4) of sectarian rivals promoting "another Jesus."

My proposal does not entail that the hypothetical non-Christian source text originated with an *anti*-Christian sect, only with one that placed Jesus on a lower rung than its own prophet. This is exactly the way John the Baptist is portrayed in John 3:26-30 and Luke 3:15-16a.

---

1 Rudolf Bultmann, *The Gospel of John: A Commentary*. Trans. G.R. Beasley-Murray, R.W.N. Hoare, and J.K. Riches (Philadelphia: Westminster Press, 1971), pp. 17-18.

2 Stanley Jerome Isser, *The Dositheans: A Samaritan Sect in Late Antiquity*. Studies in Judaism in Late Antiquity Volume Seventeen (Leiden: E.J. Brill, 1976). Pp. 53-54.

SON OF MAN: SUM OF THE MATTER

Biblical literalism, ironically, often does more to obscure the understanding of scripture than to elucidate it. One of the worst devices for (unwittingly) confusing biblical teaching is *harmonization*, a wrongheaded effort to defend the integrity of the Bible by papering over its contradictions, thus preventing our recognition of valuable clues and keys to grasping the diversity of early Christian literature and the theologies underlying it. A prime example would be the tendency to ignore the very different denotations and functions of the phrase "son of man." Of course the basic meaning is, simply, "human being." Prominent occurrences of "son of man" are found in the Psalms, Ezekiel, and Daniel 7. Sometimes "son of man" denotes "mankind" in general, speaking of the lot of all men and women, their rights, limitations, and vicissitudes. Usually the point of such references is to defend one's own case by appeal to the fact that one's rights or flaws are "common to man" (e.g., 1 Cor. 10:13).

Other times, apparently third-person "son of man" references are implicitly first-person self-references intended to tactfully "disguise" oneself in the advancing shadow of impending misfortune, as if to avert one's fate. As if avoiding explicit use of "I" or "me" might render one inconspicuous when the Grim Reaper comes looking for you.

But there is a very different use in which "son of man" occurs in an apocalyptic context. This last is not merely *based upon* the Daniel 7 vision of "one like a son of man" who defeats a series of primordial sea monsters before assuming divine co-regency alongside the Ancient of Days. The recurring allusion is not merely based on Daniel 7, I say, but is a short-hand citation of that text. This means that the apocalyptic use of "son of man" should not be (mis)understood as a title.

New Testament scholarship has long suffered from the assumption that in the gospels the phrase is always a Messianic title and that it refers to Jesus. This reading results in an erroneous gospel Christology according to which Jesus claims for himself the Messianic role and, *precisely as the incarnate Son of Man*, possesses unique authority to forgive sins and to violate Sabbath rules. *Precisely as the Danielic Son of Man* he must undergo redemptive execution, and usher in the

Final Judgment. This confusingly diverse resume is the product of the amalgamation of originally very different usages of the phrase "son of man." This composite portrait is the result of a fundamental error, all too commonly committed, namely the gratuitous assumption that a single word or phrase means the same thing in any context, any time it is used. In this way scholars have unwittingly fabricated a Messianic chimera—and identified it with Jesus. On the contrary, whenever the evangelists allude to the future advent of the Son of Man, it is only the (fictive) narrative context that implies the identification of Jesus as this Son of Man, not the individual Son of Man sayings themselves. In the Synoptic Apocalypse of Mark 13 Jesus never says that he is the prophesied Son of Man. We have always supposed otherwise because he warns the disciples (i.e., the readers) to ignore deceivers making false claims about the identity of the Son of Man. But what if these deceivers were originally intended as claiming that the coming deliverer/judge *will be a returned Jesus*? If so, the warning was not heeded, since the identification of the Son of Man as Jesus prevailed. (As we have seen, this development had already begun before the final compilation of the Gospel of John.)

If my theory is taken seriously, it will no longer be so clear that the Unificationist claim that the Lord of the Second Advent need not be Jesus himself returned to earth is "unscriptural." Is Unificationist doctrine, as its critics claim, a distortion of scripture? Rather, I should call it a restoration, even an excavation, of an earlier pre- or proto-Christian understanding still discernible among the strata of the gospel tradition.

The Retreat from Radical Prayer: The New Testament Evolution

Rabbi Zwi Chaim Yisroel [was] an Orthodox scholar of the Torah and a man who developed whining to an art unheard of in the West. Once… he was on his way to synagogue to celebrate the sacred Jewish holiday commemorating God reneging on every promise… [1]

Though Christian New Thought champions an allegorical or "spiritual" reading of scripture, it comes as a relief to some that New Thought is squarely based upon a couple of clear biblical texts understood literally. It is as if one were being invited to ascend a tall rope but allowed to climb the first few feet on a step ladder. The primary text I have in mind will be no surprise to you: Mark 11:22-24 ("And answering, Jesus says to them, 'Have faith in God. Amen: I tell you that whoever says to this mountain, "Up and into the sea with you!" and believes that what he says happens, it will be granted to him. In view of that, I tell you, all things for which you pray and ask, believe that they are yours, and your request will be granted you.'"). Upon this rock, I maintain, is built the whole edifice of "name it and claim it" prayer, "blank check" prayer. The proposition is as simple as it is radical: I ask, God grants, and I can be sure he will.

Is it a magic formula? No, for there is already an escape clause: one must believe the request will be granted. It is almost a Zen statement;[2] one must have set aside all considerations of worldly probability and expectation, as Romans 4:17-21 says Abraham did, or no heir would have been forthcoming. The logic is this: nothing shall be consid-

---

1 Woody Allen, "Hassidic Tales." In Allen, *Getting Even* (New York: Vintage Books, 1978), p. 50.

2 Joseph Chilton Pearce, *The Crack in the Cosmic Egg: Challenging Constructs of Mind and Reality* (New York: Pocket Books, 1973), pp. 176-177.

ered impossible for God. Once God enters the equation, all bets are off. Or rather, they are *on*. It is no longer either impossible or unlikely that your prayer will be realized, since it is nothing for God to do it. He will not even work up a sweat. Why *not* believe he will do it?

From this summit of believing expectation I suggest we witness a gradual decline through the pages of the New Testament, like the returning dullness of the disciples, as their stupid questions show, as they descend the Mount of Transfiguration with the no-longer glowing Jesus. We will detect clear signs of a shrinking confidence in prayer. I hope to demonstrate this decline presently, but first I propose a simple explanation (or two) for it. What we are witnessing in this retreat from radical prayer is the cooling of sectarian zeal typical for all new religious movements. As time goes by, once-sizzling believers sink back into complacent conformity with the norms of the society and religion against which they first stood out like a sore thumb. One cannot maintain fever-pitch zeal forever as long as one must live in a world that is not evidently coming to a crashing end in the near future. There are bills to pay, family to be provided for, civic obligations to mind. Religion retreats to a sideline, a hobby, a pursuit to which one regrets one cannot devote more energy. If a select few want to maintain their "first love" in all its fervor, there will be special arrangements for them: monasteries, convents, etc. These are special environments mimicking the Kingdom of God these few wish they lived in, with no worldly distractions, like the Holodeck on *Star Trek*.

Everyone else retreats to a stance that Reinhold Niebuhr called "Christian Realism." It proves impractical to heed literally those radical gospel mandates including non-retaliation in wartime, abandoning worldly security, donating all worldly goods to the poor (thereby joining their number, along with one's family who probably weren't in on the decision!). With the compromises one forfeits the old confidence in promises (real or imagined) of prayer for healing, for sinless sanctification, for Spirit-inspired boldness in witnessing. All these come to be thought of as "relevant but impossible ideals." They play the role of the North Star: guiding the way, but not in itself a credible destination. One is too much in the world to live every day in the fantasy world of a Jesus movie. Perhaps the closest New Testament parallel to the retreat from radical prayer would be the early expectation of the Parousia, the second coming of Christ. We start with gospel promises that the end will dawn before the generation of Jesus' contemporaries has expired: Mark 13:30, "This generation will not pass away till all these things are fulfilled." But time went by and nothing happened. Many died. So now we read a hedged version of the promise: "*Some* standing here will not taste death till they see the kingdom of God having come with power" (Mark 9:1). Eventually the available witness pool shrank to one single survivor: "It was rumored among the brethren that this disciple was not to die" (John 21:23a). But then he died, and it was time to reinterpret the promise again! "But Jesus did not actually *say* he was not going to die, only that if he so willed, it was no one else's business" (John 21:23b). And then the ridicule set in with a vengeance: "First of all, be sure of this: *in the last days, mockers will appear, following their own lusts*, making wisecracks, saying things like, 'What happened to the promise of his coming? After all, from the day the fathers fell asleep, all remains as it was since the dawn of creation!'" (2 Peter 3:3-4). The answer? "But, brothers, don't you let this fact be concealed from you: 'One day for the Lord is the same as a millennium, and a millennium as a single day.' It is not so much that the Lord is tardy fulfilling his promise, as some define tardiness. No, it is that he is long-suffering toward you, unwilling for any to perish and hoping everyone will come to their senses" (2 Peter 3:8-9). Sure, it's a delay, wiseass, but you ought to be grateful for it! It's a reprieve! Not bad reasoning, but the tendency is nonetheless clear: a retreat from imminent expectation of the Parousia to the calm belief that, yes, it will happen *some* day. In the meantime, don't take advantage of the delay. Don't give up hope. This is the point of the parables of the Lazy Steward (Matthew 24:45-51) and the Wise and Foolish Virgins (Matthew 25:1-13).

Another parallel: think of Mark 9:28-29, "And when [after an exorcism,] he entered into a house, his disciples questioned him privately: 'Why were we unable to cast it out?' And he told them. 'This particular species can come out by means of nothing but prayer. [And, if that doesn't work, fasting].'" The story came to be used in the early church as a formula for exorcism,[1] but mere recitation of the story of Jesus' triumph did not do the trick after a while (if it ever had), so someone started fine-tuning, adding *prayer* as a condition for success with deaf-mute epilepsy demons. When this, too, proved ineffective after a while, some scribes began to add the stipulation of *fasting* for the exorcist-in-training before "the big match." It is the same sort of pious back- pedaling we are gauging with prayer.

Even closer, though from another religious tradition, would be the failure of Shankara's promise that simple understanding of the major Upanishadic statements of Nondualism must issue in immediate enlightenment. It turned out not to be so simple:

> Samkaracarya declared that the cognitive understanding of the meaning of the four great Upanisadic dicta, 'this *atma* is *brahma*', 'I am *brahma*', 'thou art that', and 'the conscious self is *brahma*', results in immediate liberation. Most of his contemporaries and particularly his later opponents... opposed this notion vehemently, insisting on prolonged observance and discipline."[2]

Why? Obviously because, even though some people managed to understand the concept of the thing, nothing happened. The promised enlightenment, a mystical experience of one's unity with the Godhead, did not occur. Thus many decided some further steps must be necessary to clear away the clouds of worldly ignorance.[3] I said there is a second reason for the decline from religious radicalism, and that is,

---

1 Stevan L. Davies, *The Revolt of the Widows: The Social World of the Apocryphal Acts* (Carbondale: Southern Illinois University Press, 1980), pp. 22-23, referring to Origen, *Contra Celsum* 1.46. See also Raphael Patai, *The Hebrew Goddess* (New York: Avon/Discus Books, 1978), pp. 188-189, for the similar use of Elijah stories in medieval Jewish exorcism rites.

2 Agehananda Bharati, *The Tantric Tradition* (Garden City: Doubleday Anchor Books, 1970), pp. 19-20.

3 See L. Thomas O'Neil, *Maya in Sankara: Measuring the Immeasurable* (Dehli: Motilal Banarsidass, 1980), Chapter Five, "Maya in the Post-Sankara Advaita," pp. 96-124.

as a skeptic would say, *a gradual coming to terms with reality*. The exper-
iment of faith just fails, and one learns the lesson ruefully. Henceforth
one's expectations are not so great. One whittles down the promises
enough that even tepid faith may grasp them, not that there is much
pay-off to be had. One tells oneself that it was never realistic to expect
entire sanctification, miraculous healing, not to grow old, to survive
till the second coming, to be provided for even after giving away all
one's money, to go out onto the field of battle and be invulnerable to
the unbelievers' bullets.[1] Wise up.

Of course, from the believer's standpoint, this is not an awakening
to mature realism at all. The true believer will lament that faith has
been lost, and with it great treasures to which it might have been the
key. I guess the difference between the two stances is one's track record:
how many times has the believed-for blessing fallen through? But then
the question passes over into *theodicy*: can we think of ways to absolve
God of the apparent failure of his promises? To make it *our* fault? What
we are about to see in our brief survey of other New Testament texts
on faith and prayer is a series of *mitigations* of the original promises,
the addition of stipulations, provisos, and conditions. The reason they
have been added is to vindicate God in the face of the failure of believing prayer. Sure, confidence in prayer is thereby undermined, but even
that is better than blaming God. One Psalm demands to know: "Why
sleepest thou, O Lord?" Another replies, No, "He that guardeth Israel
neither slumbers nor sleeps."

I must observe that even the repeated delay of the Parousia, like the
failure of prayer, has been explained as due to the failure of believers,
not of God. This is the point of Acts 3:19-21 ("So repent and turn back,
for your sins to be expunged, so times of restoration may arrive from
the presence of the Lord and he may send the Christ already appointed

---

1 Most famous as occurring in the Boxer Rebellion in China, this belief in
   charismatic invulnerability occurs also in several Asian Indian messianic
   movements. See Stephen Fuchs, *Rebellious Prophets: A Study of Messianic
   Movements in Indian Religions*. Publications of the Indian Branch of the
   Anthropos Institute No. 1 (New York: Asia Publishing House, 1965), pp.
   29-30, 32, 41, 96, 98, 107, 123, 149-150, 220.

for you, Jesus, whom heaven is required to keep until times of restitu-
tion of all things, which God spoke about through the mouth of all his
holy prophets from antiquity"). If Christ has not returned on sched-
ule it is *our* fault. This is an old notion inherited from Judaism: why
does the Messiah not come to relieve Jewish suffering? Because they do
not show themselves worthy of his deliverance by keeping the Torah.

MUSTARD SEED OF DOUBT

To repeat: a second look at Mark 11:22-24: "Have faith in God. Amen:
I tell you that whoever says to this mountain, 'Up and into the sea with
you!' and believes that what he says happens, it will be granted to him.
In view of that, I tell you, all things for which you pray and ask, believe
that they are yours, and your request will be granted you." It suggests
that an escape clause has already been inserted to mitigate the easily-
disproven boast of the original promise. "And does not doubt in his
heart." This condition seems to introduce the element of doubt, inject-
ing a taint into the absolute confidence the saying otherwise means to
encourage. One problem is that this condition fatally shifts the focus
from what an omnipotent God may do on the one hand, to a mortal's
faith on the other. If the believer can muster up enough faith, like Green
Lantern summoning up sufficient will power to operate his power
ring, he will accomplish the miracle. The believer has replaced God as
the wonder-worker. He is answering his own prayer. The pious reader
stumbles at the challenge of mountain-moving power and inevitably
asks, "Do I have enough faith for *that*? *Could* I?" This is an element
of fearful introspection (familiar, I do not doubt, to every one who
has ever taken this promise seriously). It saps the pure confidence with
which Superman makes his leap from the open window of the Daily
Planet. When Yoda upbraids Luke Skywalker, telling him that he must
not *try* to raise his vehicle from the swamp, that instead he must simply
do it, he is telling Luke to exorcize that poisonous element of doubt.
But Mark 11:23, as I read it, injects the mustard seed, not of *faith*, but
of *doubt*, preparing the reader in advance for failure. James 1:6-8 sets
up the same booby trap: "Only let him be sure to ask in faith, without
ambivalence; for the doubter wavers like the tossing of the sea, driven

and tossed by the wind. Such a one need not imagine he is likely to receive anything at all from the Lord, for he is of two minds, habitually indecisive." In the face of this sapping of the positivity of faith, one can only repeat the despairing words of the nameless man in Mark 9:24: "I'm trying to believe! Help my unbelief!"[1] At least, as in C.S. Lewis's *The Screwtape Letters*, that puts an end to the vexing doublethink.[2]

The sort of anxiety I have in mind is exactly paralleled in the agonizing of Pure Land Buddhists who had been taught they need only call upon the name of Amitabha Buddha to guarantee rebirth in the Pure Land, a Buddha-planet created through the good karma of the immortal Bodhisattva where one might attain full enlightenment at once upon arrival there. But any idiot could repeat the words "I call upon Amitabha Buddha." Mustn't there be some special state of mind? Pure Land theoreticians began the long process of debating how much desire for rebirth, how much sorrow for sins, and how much sincerity were required for the meditative recipe to work.[3] Alas, no peace of mind lies *that* way. The same Hall of Mirrors beckons us in John 15:7 ("If you dwell in me and my words dwell in you, ask whatever you wish, and it shall happen for you."): how do you know when and how fully you are dwelling "in Jesus"? Or that his sayings are dwelling, gestating, within your soul? Apparently not deeply enough if your prayers fail. It is a sliding scale that can slide as far as needed to get God off the hook.

OUTVOTING GOD

Matthew 18:19-20 says, "Again, I say to you that if two of you agree on earth concerning everything they may ask, it shall happen for them from my Father in the heavens. For where two or three are assembled

---

1 Here is what I judge the most profound New Testament saying on prayer, and who said it? Jesus? An apostle? A prophet? No, just—*some guy!*

2 C.S. Lewis, *The Screwtape Letters* (New York: Macmillan, 1970), pp. 62-63.

3 Alfred Bloom, *Shinran's Gospel of Pure Grace*. Monographs of the Association for Asian Studies (Tucson: University of Arizona Press, 1977), throughout.

in my name, I am there in their midst." The verse now forms part of a section of Matthew's gospel devoted to disciplinary matters in the local Christian community. It has much in common with the Dead Sea Scroll called the Community Rule (or Manual of Discipline). As such it must be taken as meaning that disciplinary decisions must be by consensus of a small quorum of two or three, modeled upon the Old Testament requirement of two or three witnesses (Deuteronomy 17:6; 19:15). But it is evident that the saying originally circulated as an independent pericope (a self-contained unit of oral tradition), and it concerned prayer in general. As such it forms another stage of retrenchment in prayer. It introduces another variable upon which failure in prayer may be blamed: did you have enough signatures on the petition to persuade God? This proviso gets God off the hook in one sense (he did not merely *refuse* the earnest prayer), but it implicates him in another: must God be persuaded by numbers, like the mob whose numbers persuaded Pilate to deliver Jesus unto death? That seems the most blatant superstition. But most do not notice this since their attention is naturally taken up with the more obvious feelings of solidarity and mutual support inculcated when one asks others to pray on one's behalf.

THE NAME GAME

Notice that the two or three believers assembled must have gathered "in my name," a stipulation that implies they have invoked the presence of Jesus in prayer before they started. Another variable! One might easily forget to do this. Something like this stipulation appears in a string of Johannine parallels to Mark 11:22-24. They include John 13:16 ("It was not you who chose to follow me, but I who chose you and appointed you to go forth and bear fruit, and for that fruit to remain till harvest, so that whatever you may *ask the Father in my name* he may give you."); 14:12-14, 24 ("Amen, amen: I tell you, whoever believes in me, the deeds I do, he, too, shall perform; even greater than these will he do, for I am going to the Father and someone must do them. And whatever you *ask in my name*, this I will do, that the Father may be glorified in the Son. If you *ask me anything in my name*, I will do it."); 16:23b-24 ("Amen, amen: I tell you, whatever you *request of the Father in my name*, he will give you. Up to now you *requested nothing in my name*; go ahead: ask, and you will receive, so that your joy may be undiluted by any sense of lack."). Here it has become explicit: just as James 4:2b-3a says, "You do not have for the simple reason that you do not ask! Then you ask and do not receive, because you ask wrongly." And there must be fifty ways to ask wrongly, only one to ask rightly, and who can be sure what *that* is? What exactly does it mean to pray "in Jesus' name"?

Admittedly, it might imply a blank check with Jesus' name signed to it, guaranteeing an answer. But the fact that it modifies the simple act of praying, requesting, i.e., simply in one's *own* name, subordinates prayer to Christology, imposing the creed as a presupposition for effective prayer.

COME BACK TOMORROW!

Persistence is made the condition for effectual prayer in Matthew 7:7-8 ("Just ask! It shall be given you! Look for it! You will find it! Knock, and the door will swing wide for you! For every persistent asker receives, and every determined seeker finds, and for the insistent knocker it shall sooner or later be opened"). But who does not by now recognize this saying rather as a way of discounting the criticism that prayer just did not work? "I prayed and nothing happened." But did you pray *long enough*? Who told you that you can hold God to a deadline? It is like the Eight-Ball toy which pretends to answer someone's query, "Will I get a mate?" with the "answer" of "Ask again" or "The future will disclose it." It is a way of saying that an immediate, timely answer may *never* come, and you will have no right to complain. The answer, for all you may know, might have arrived the day after you gave up.

GOD SAYS NO

Matthew 7:9-11 says, "Just point out a man among you who would give his son a rock if he asked him for a roll! Or, if he asked for a fish, who would give him a snake? And if you, being sinners, nonetheless know to give good gifts to your children, how much more can you expect your Father in the heavens to give good things to those who ask him?" At first this passage seems to persuade with sweet reason that one ought to expect God, as a compassionate father, to come forward with what one needs. After all, why on earth *wouldn't* he? And yet even here we detect an implication of the opposite: suppose the child, little realizing the consequences, were to ask Dad for a tasty-looking rock or a pretty snake? We must assume a good father would withhold these items rather than making his son learn his lesson the hard way, which presumably explains why God declined to grant you that relationship or that job you were praying for.

Romans 8:26-27 reads: "The Spirit, too, takes a hand in our weakness: while we do not know our own good well enough to ask for it, the Spirit itself intercedes on our behalf with inarticulate groanings; with the result that the Searcher of hearts knows the thinking of the Spirit, because he is able to ask on behalf of the saints from God's perspective." This text provides the same evasion. To wit, why do we fail to receive that for which we beseech God time and time again? Simply because God sees the big picture that we cannot see, and he knows that sometimes to grant our requests would be like the wishes granted with perverse irony in "The Monkey's Paw."

We may find that a prayer goes unanswered and never learn why (though it is usually pretty easy to come up with a few guesses), but then again we may learn that the good we had hoped to receive was in reality the enemy of the best God had for us, as Paul found out the hard way in 2 Corinthians 12:7-9 ("To prevent me from becoming swell-headed over the superabundance of revelations vouchsafed me, a thorn in the flesh was given me, an angel of the Accuser, to punish me, to prevent my self-inflation. I pleaded with the Lord three times about this, that I might become free of it. And he said to me, 'My charisma is sufficient for you, for my power is perfected in weakness.'" I'm not giving you what's behind Door Number One, Paul, because I've seen what's behind Door Number Two, and, believe me, it's a whole lot better!" Who's going to complain about that?

There is nothing at all unreasonable about this explanation. It makes plenty of sense. That is not the point. It is just that, if one were mindful of these considerations *going in*, one would scarcely have the effrontery to "claim" or "demand" things from God or even to "believe God" for this or that. We ought to envision the possibility of "No" as an answer right up front.

PRAYER WARRIORS

As early sectarian Christianity began to settle back into conformity with worldly values and to expect less of God (rightly or wrongly!), those challenges once issued to all within earshot ("Sell your possessions! Leave your family and wander the roads preaching! Take up the martyr's cross! Cast out demons! Heal the sick! Speak in new tongues! It is good for a man not to touch a woman!")—they were reduced in application to a sacred elite of "hundred per centers," with everybody else let off the hook. Such is the context of 1 Corinthians chapter 13, where what were at first marks of *all* Jesus' followers have now become spiritual gifts found only among a select and celebrated few: the charismatic itinerant preachers, the celibate orders of widows and virgins, the exorcists, healers, martyrs and confessors, and prophets. Note how that in 1 Corinthians 13:1-3 mountain-moving faith has become a super-power of only such an elite, no longer expected of all believers: "If I speak in human tongues and those of angels, but I have not love, I am merely making noise, like a trumpet blast or a crashing cymbal. If I have the mantel of prophecy and know all mysteries and all *gnosis*, and if I have complete faith so as to be able to uproot mountains at a word, but I have not love, I am nothing. And if I donate all my possessions, and if I deliver up my body to be burnt, but I have not love, I gain no heavenly reward by it." Need I say it? This is yet another way to evade the demand for radical prayer and faith, to legitimatize tepid faith. Only Christian superheroes have faith like *that*!

DREAM CATCH 22

The penultimate position on the New Testament scale of prayer is occupied by 1 John 5:14: "And this is the confidence we have in him, that if we ask anything according to his will he hears us." It sounds as if we were back all at once breathing the rarified mountaintop air of Mark 11:22-24 again! But we are not. Now there is, attached like a barnacle to the hull of the promise, the proviso that only prayers which happen to accord with *what God already* had planned will be answered. Which is to say they are not answered at all, since petitioning God is moot. His will is set. If our requests happen to match it, good for us. If they don't, too bad. That sober realism we have already come to understand. But now the dilemma becomes crystal clear: *why pray at all?*

Take the case of Jesus in Gethsemane. He prays to his Father: "All things are possible for you. Let this cup pass from me; nevertheless, your will be done, not mine." Jesus lets his preference be known. But he yields to God's plan, for ultimately he shares what Immanuel Kant called "the holy will of God"—to prize one's duty above all else. But then would it not be more consistent to abbreviate the whole process, as Meister Eckhardt counseled? To pray nothing but "Thy will be done," the goal being, not to alter God's plan (as if poor mortals might point out a better way to him!), but rather simply to align one's own will with God's infinite wisdom? Why ask anything at all?

> What is the prayer of the disinterested heart? I answer by saying that a disinterested man, pure in heart, has no prayer, for to pray is to want something from God, something added that one desires, or something that God is to take away. The disinterested person, however, wants nothing, and neither has he anything of which he would be rid. Therefore he has no prayer, or he prays only to be uniform with God.[1]

I think this is one of those places where, as Paul Tillich said, the Bible raises a philosophical question that it does not answer in philosophical terms. "If one starts to think about the meaning of biblical symbols, one is already in the midst of ontological problems."[2] Scripture

---

1 Meister Eckhardt, "About Disinterest," in *Meister Eckhardt: A Modern Translation*. Trans. Raymond B. Blakney (New York: Harper & Row, 1941), pp. 88-89.

2 Paul Tillich, *Biblical Religion and the Search for Ultimate Reality* (Chicago: University of Chicago Press, 1972), p. 83.

raises the philosophical questions and leaves it to us to answer them. And this means that what it says about prayer finally points toward the dissolution of prayer in *pure surrender*. And this will mean that earlier New Testament passages about prayer, the ones we began with, must yield to the final insight, to be discarded, much as Shankara said all prayers, hymns, and devotions are moot once one comes to realize one's identity with the Godhead. That, in turn, is why in the Gospel of Thomas, saying 14, Jesus warns: "If you fast, you will only engender sin for yourselves. And if you pray, you will be damned. And if you give alms, you will only do your spirit harm."

NO MORE BAIT AND SWITCH

I have tried to outline the process by which the initial absolute confidence of radical prayer gave way to tepid half-belief like that of King Ahaz in Isaiah 14 who lacked the spine to name a sign for Jehovah to perform for him. One proviso, one condition, one bit of fine print after another finally whittled away that radical faith until in the end all such faith, assuming as it did a privileged knowledge of the secret will of God that no mortal possesses, dissolved into surrender. Seen this way, petitionary prayer turns out to be a cocoon from which a kind of Taoist passivity emerges like a butterfly. It would mean petitionary prayer is a childish thing to be transcended by the mature.

But is it? It is too easy to sacrifice familiar religious experiences to the unfeeling logic of systematic theology. Accordingly, I hesitate simply to cut loose biblical personalism, the notion, at bottom, that there is somehow Someone listening to us. Your spirit may indeed be willing to rest in utter submission to God and God's will, but your heart cries out to God nonetheless, and theology shouldn't stop you. And if this is where we find ourselves, what else can we learn from our survey of faith promises and their mitigation?

It is the lesson of the Three Young Men in the fiery furnace. "Our God, whom we serve, is able to deliver us from the burning fiery furnace; and he will deliver us out of your clutches, O king. But if not, know this, O king: we will not serve your gods or bow before the golden image you erected" (Daniel 3:17-18). This seems to me to be the perfect attitude of prayer. One can pray in confidence that God can do anything he pleases, including answering one's specific prayer. But being a puny mortal, one does not presume to know God's will in every situation. He may have his own reasons for not answering, and that is his business. The attitude of Shadrach, Meshach, and Abed-Nego was *confidence without presumption*. It is the sheer faith that God can do anything, together with the Socratic humility to admit one cannot know what God will choose to do. That humility is not doubt. It is only to recognize the freedom of God to do anything, to act "outside the box" in which we seek to trap him when we dictate alternatives to him in our prayers.

The error of prayer we have seen to be a misplaced confidence, not in the power of God, but in our ability to know what he would want to do. One thing is safe to say we know, though: if we reduce God to a genie beholden to our whims, we have created an idol who will never hear our prayers or anything else.

The Theological Tragedy of George Eldon Ladd

I have just finished reading John A. D'Elia's *A Place at the Table: George Eldon Ladd and the Rehabilitation of Evangelical Scholarship in America*, a fascinating biography of the dean of evangelical New Testament scholars. George E. Ladd (1911-1982) was a pivotal figure in the 1940s-60s attempt of the so-called Neo-Evangelicals to escape the self-imposed prison of irrelevance in which conservative Protestants had languished ever since the Fundamentalist-Modernist Controversies at the turn of the century and in the 1920s in which the major denominations were split between advocates of the Old Time Religion and those who sought to accommodate the faith to new learning. Cooperative efforts between liberals and conservatives were henceforth rendered impossible. Not only that, but, if you weren't a Fundamentalist, you probably thought Fundamentalists were backward-looking, obscurantist fanatics. Worse yet, confined to an intellectual ghetto of their own making, Fundamentalists sharpened their swords in combat with one another in a series of ongoing internecine doctrinal squabbles. The Baptists in particular were divided over the fine print of eschatology: the doctrine of the impending end of the world and the second coming of Christ.

Astonishing as it seems to outsiders (even if we began as insiders), the Baptists, Plymouth Brethren, and others made "Pretribulationism" the touchstone of orthodoxy. It was deemed vitally important that one should believe that the Rapture (the ascension of all true Christians to meet a hovering Jesus in the stratosphere and then accompany him to heaven) must occur on the eve of the Great Tribulation and the reign of the Antichrist, no later, for Christians must not be put through the ensuing horrors. The major alternative was "Posttribulationism," which scheduled the Rapture (what Fuller Seminary Professor Arthur Glasser would later scoffingly refer to as "the cosmic Dunkirk") *after* the

Tribulation. "Posttribbers" urged Christians to swallow hard and get ready for rough weather ahead. (I remember these controversies still being alive in the 1970s.)

This all seems tantamount to a slap fight between Jehovah's Witnesses. And a vanguard of "New Evangelicals" led by Carl F. H. Henry, Harold John Ockenga, Billy Graham, Harold Lindsell (all of whom I had the honor of meeting in person), Gordon Clark, Bernard Ramm, and others, couldn't stop cringing. They had wider cultural sympathies and bemoaned the fact that Fundamentalists had made such a laughingstock of their own religion. These men, themselves very conservative theologically, wanted to reintegrate evangelicalism into the socio-cultural mainstream. They wanted respect both for their style of Christianity and for themselves. One can scarcely blame them. They let it be known that they eagerly sought dialogue with theological liberals and mainstream biblical scholars. George Ladd was the major Neo-Evangelical to emerge in New Testament studies.

Ladd, sadly, sacrificed any happy family life to his all-consuming quest to achieve "a place at the table" of legitimate, respectable, critical scholars, which at the time included Rudolf Bultmann, Günther Bornkamm, Norman Perrin, and Oscar Cullmann. Ladd earned a Ph.D degree at Harvard under the great New Testament scholar Henry J. Cadbury, and soon found a position at Gordon Divinity School (now Gordon-Conwell Theological Seminary, my own alma mater). During an initial period of debating and debunking Pretribulationalists (also called Dispensationalists), Ladd succeeded in distinguishing himself from the cultish world of doctrinaire Fundamentalism. This is another way of saying he had become marginalized in their circles, but that was fine with him: he had better things in mind. Namely, Ladd wanted to secure the standing of a genuine colleague. He still had plenty to criticize in critical scholarship, but he committed himself to do it by way of cordial and respectful dialogue, not via polemics. That's the way to win friends and influence people, after all. He hoped, almost single-handedly, to win respect for conservative scholarship. But he wanted to recruit and train other like-minded, intellectually curious evangelicals to join him, and in this he was quite successful.

Ladd's first books addressed intra-evangelical issues and appeared from Evangelical publishers (like Eerdmans and InterVarsity), but he felt he had really arrived when Harper & Row contracted to issue his magnum opus, *Jesus and the Kingdom*, a study of New Testament eschatology and the discussion of it among, not fundamentalist prophecy-geeks, but mainstream scholars. Ladd was riding high—until the very first review of his book punctured his balloon with a loud pop. Norman Perrin, a radical Bultmannian, excoriated Ladd's book. Other reviews were kinder, but this one embittered Ladd for the rest of his life, convincing him that his dream of evangelicals joining the critical mainstream had been a pathetic delusion. He decided henceforth to barricade himself safely behind the walls of Neo-Evangelicalism, his natural home. Ladd had been influenced by the most conservative of mainstream critics, Cullmann, and had even praised certain aspects of Bultmann's thought (while keeping his distance well away from the latter's controversial demythologizing program). But he was still solidly (Neo-) Evangelical.

Ladd's disappointments warped his perspective. Subsequent invitations to speak and write for mainstream scholarly venues proved that he *had* attained his goal of collegial respect, though he was blind to it. And he certainly turned out to be an Abraham whose scholarly descendants can hardly be numbered.

But Ladd's experiences highlight an important issue. Perrin's critique, though apparently pretty nasty, was on point. Ladd was just too darn easy on himself methodologically by accepting pretty much any and every Synoptic saying of Jesus as authentic. He took all the Jesus stories as historical, too. And this transparently because of his Evangelical doctrine of an infallible scripture. In his attempt to get as close to the Bultmannians as he could without getting infected, he was admittedly negotiating between what his theology needed (i.e., for Jesus' resurrection to have been an actual historical occurrence) and the notion of *geschichtliche* (supra-historical) "events." In short, he was putting forth a slate of parochial exegesis, controlled by theological constraints. His attempt to play footsy with liberal academics was less a scholarly exchange (though Ladd was a true and great scholar; I must have read, let me see, at least seven of his books) than an ecumenical dialogue between different faith positions. A twin problem was that his stance had the inevitable effect of reducing his whole scholarly enterprise to an exercise in bowdlerization, picking through mainstream scholarship to appropriate what bits and pieces he could adapt to parochial evangelical sensibilities. Form criticism? Okay, as long as we don't infer from it that some gospel materials are inauthentic. No, the Holy Spirit might have, therefore *must* have, preserved the Jesus tradition accurately. You get the idea. The result is a kind of Special Olympics of biblical criticism. Read enough books of this type and you start suspecting that "progressive Evangelicals" do not really want to learn too much, lest it upset the apple cart. Worse still, they flirt with critical scholarship in order to opportunistically turn it against genuine criticism. Conservative biblical scholarship turns out to be a euphemism for apologetics. Today we recognize writers such as Ben Witherington III and N.T. Wright as axe-grinding apologists in sheep's clothing.

There is gossip in D'Elia's book, but there is no point in suppressing it, especially since it is theologically relevant. I have already mentioned Ladd's pathological, self-destructive resentments, his brittle self-esteem, etc. These are transparently the results of Ladd's difficult childhood, at home and at school, and his inability to give or to receive love. Eventually Ladd descended into alcoholism and sexual indiscretions. He found what solace he could in the bottle and on the psychiatrist's couch. In other words, not from sweet fellowship with the Savior. It is easy for those of us who have repudiated Fundamentalism and Evangelicalism to gloat over such failings on the part of a man like George Ladd, though such *Schadenfreude* is adolescent and unworthy. But it *is* significant that so pious a man as Ladd, zealous for his creed, for prayer, for missionary evangelism, could not walk the walk. Let us not commit the hasty generalization fallacy and make Ladd the face of Evangelicals as a whole. But on the other hand, the case is not too far removed from the time the skinny guru of the "Breatharian" movement who taught that one need only imbibe fruit juice and clean air, was found in an all-night diner munching cheeseburgers. If the guy who knows the thing best and crows about it the loudest turns out not to be able to make it work, it just shatters the credibility of the product he's selling. It is so important to safeguard the gospel message of a transformed, regenerated, Christ-sanctified life that we must reject any critical theories of the Bible that might undermine such a belief— *and it doesn't even work.* George Ladd's life teaches us more about his beloved Christian gospel than he realized, both good and bad.

Toward a Legalistic Understanding of the Sermon on the Mount

It is almost humorous that the question should be asked: "Are we expected to keep the precepts of the Sermon on the Mount?" Yet this question lies behind the long history of serious controversy over the Sermon's purpose. Are we to meet its high standards, and if so, what is at stake? The Lutheran interpretation of the Sermon reads it through the spectacles of the Law-Grace dialectic; the Sermon is an intentionally impossible statement of moral principal designed to crush us into despair: "O wretched man that I am! Who will deliver me?" The Dispensationalist interpretation somehow manages to defer the Sermon to the Millennial Kingdom. While Christians today may find valid moral guidance there, the Sermon is really addressed to another time: "Don't open till Christmas." The "interim-ethic" perspective sees the Sermon as emergency measures for the end of the age: "What to do till the Messiah comes," sort of ethical Flagellism. The imagined crisis has evaporated, however, and Christians may look elsewhere for ethical instructions.[1]

A more recent view as propounded, e.g., by A.M. Hunter and Joachim Jeremias, sees the Sermon as a charter for life in the inaugurated Kingdom of Heaven, presupposing that such a Kingdom has arrived.[2] Seen in this way, the Sermon's demands are to be obeyed ("Je-

---

1 It may be questioned whether Albert Schweitzer was quite as glib about this as many seem to think. See his discussion of the interim-ethic in *The Mystery of the Kingdom of God*. Trans. Walter Lowrie (New York: Schocken Books, 1964), p. 103.

2 Archibald M. Hunter, *A Pattern for Life* (Philadelphia: Westminster Press, 1976), pp. 16, 17, 104-105; Joachim Jeremias, *The Sermon on the Mount.* Trans. Norman Perrin. Facet Books, Biblical Series 2 (Philadelphia: Fortress Press, 1975), pp. 30 ff.

sus… does not hesitate to use the imperative, 'You must.'"),[1] but *not* "in the sense that they [the demands] say: 'You must do all of this, in order that you may be saved.'"[2] Indeed, that last seems to be the alternative that everyone wants to avoid at all costs! This is the "perfectionist" or "legalistic" interpretation. One almost suspects that exegetes scurry to avoid this interpretation because of the embarrassment (to put it mildly) that it would occasion. If the Sermon is intended this way, the Pauline Christian feels doomed! He thinks that he can never hope to live up to the Sermon. Surely Jesus knew this! But suppose he didn't! What exegete wants to end up thinking he is doomed, or otherwise, that he knows better than Jesus? So the Sermon *isn't* intended legalistically, because it just *can't* be! But no, the exegete must be prepared to find anything in the text, no matter how unbelievable or fanatical it may seem. There is no room here for dogmatic or pietistic vested interests.

It will be the suggestion of this paper that the Sermon is best understood legalistically. The main direction to be pursued will be that of the nature of the Sermon's principles as demands, especially in the context of threatened punishments and promised rewards. There will follow a brief examination of the Sermon's attitude toward the keeping of the Jewish Law.

First it must be observed that the proper object of our study is *Matthew's* Sermon on the Mount. The discourse, as is generally recognized, is in its present form Matthew's work, a compilation of sayings spoken by Jesus, if at all, on different occasions. What is often overlooked, however, is that attention must also be paid to the position of the Sermon in the gospel account as presently structured by the evangelist. In fact, it is only in disregard of this crucial fact that exegetes have been able to presuppose a background of previous preaching of the Kingdom. For instance, Bruce Metzger suggests the necessity of not locating the Sermon too early in the ministry of Jesus since its teaching is too advanced, presupposing the previous call of the disciples *into the Kingdom*, i.e., not simply as disciples of Jesus.[3] However,

---

1 Jeremias, *Sermon on the Mount*, p. 32.

2 Ibid. p. 34.

3 Class lecture.

this is to interpret the Sermon in accord with a hypothetical "life-of-Jesus" construct instead of in the framework of Matthew. Here, as the initial sermon of Jesus, it functions as the introduction to Jesus' message, much as the Nazareth sermon in Luke 4 obviously functions as the keynote, programmatic speech by virtue of its (artificial) placement in the narrative as much as by its content.

Jeremias makes the same sort of error by isolating the Sermon as a piece of early Christian catechesis, i.e., addressed to those already safely in the Kingdom. He says quite plainly: "The instructions of the Sermon have been torn out of their original context … All of them are, as it were, apodoses, which cannot be understood without the protasis … The Sermon on the Mount—ostensibly—retains only the apodoses and leaves out the protasis."[1] In other words, one cannot correctly understand the Sermon as it stands in the text! In fact, if left with the text alone, one must arrive at the very opposite conclusion of what it supposedly intended![2] Jeremias sees the Sermon as a collection of examples of lived faith for those already in the present Kingdom. The present paper will seek to demonstrate that the theology of the Gospel of Matthew does not allow for such a presupposed present Kingdom, and that the wording of the Sermon itself forces its demands to be understood as requirements, not examples.

First it must be asked, does the Gospel of Matthew teach the presence of the Kingdom of Heaven? A brief survey of relevant passages is in order. By far the largest number of Kingdom sayings clearly speak of it as an eschatological future entity: 3:2; 5:19-20; 6:10; 8:11; 10:7; 16:28; 18:1-4; 20:21; 26:29. There are, of course, other sayings interpreted by some to teach a presence of the Kingdom. However, each of these is very problematic or can easily be understood as referring to the future Kingdom.

---

1 Jeremias, *Sermon on the Mount*, pp. 30-31.

2 Indeed, it is no exaggeration to compare what Jeremias says here with the old joke in which one guy says, "Didja know the Bible teaches atheism?" His pal answers, "Yeah? Where does it say that?" The first guy says, "Right here: 'There is no God.'" The second guy points out that the whole verse is "*The fool has said in his heart,* 'There is no God.'" Oops.

Two of the Beatitudes call their subjects blessed for theirs *is* the Kingdom. However, this is probably meant in a promissory sense. They are assured of inheriting the Kingdom when it comes, just as the other promised blessings refer to the coming eschatological reversals. It has been suggested that the subjects spoken of in the Beatitudes represent different aspects of one kind of person, the kind who will enter the Kingdom. Surely this is true as well of the promised blessings. They are all of a piece, and thus all future. But what of the present state of "blessedness" ascribed to the poor in spirit, the meek, etc.? Does this not imply a present new order of spiritual ("eschatological") joy? This would press too much meaning into the beatitude form in which the blessedness is equivalent to a guarantee of *future* joy to those now suffering.[1] "They, contrary to appearance, are the lucky ones!" The blessedness, defined by the *hoti* clauses, is a promise for the future.

It has been claimed that Jesus' allusion to Isaiah 35:5 in answer to John the Baptist's question in Matthew 11:2-6 means that the Messianic Kingdom is here! This, however, is too hasty a reading. As John's question is framed, the issue is, "Is Jesus the Coming One?" not "Is the Kingdom here?" The enumerated signs are Jesus' credentials. John is warned not to take offense at *him*, not at the Kingdom. That the Kingdom is not present should be clear. Jesus is the one who will bring it, but he is not necessarily doing it at the time he is saying these words. The original Isaiah passage concerns the new order of salvation, but Jesus modifies it by including among the eschatological signs the preaching of the gospel. In Matthew this means the gospel of the kingdom (e.g., 9:35), which is the announcement of the imminent but future advent of the Kingdom (cf. 10:7). Thus Isaiah's description of the presence of the new age is applied by Jesus to describe the signs of its near (though future) approach instead.

But in the same passage, does not Jesus describe the shift of aeons since John? The Law and the Prophets prophesied until John, so this must be the new time in which the Law and the Prophets are super-

---

1 Cf. Klaus Koch, *The Growth of the Biblical Tradition: The Form-Critical Method.* Trans. S.M. Cupitt. Scribner Studies in Biblical Interpretation (New York: Scribners, 1969), pp. 17-18.

seded. No, all the statement means is that the prediction of Elijah's return (now fulfilled in John) stood as the last thing in the Hebrew division of Law and Prophets.[1] This says nothing about a new order of the supersession of the Law. What of the "violence" connected with the Kingdom in the same verse? This is perhaps best understood as a reference to the violence perpetrated by Herod Antipas upon John as the Kingdom's herald. However, George E. Ladd's attempt to understand the sentence as "The Kingdom of Heaven acts powerfully"[2] might be correct. A similar conjecture is, "The Kingdom of Heaven advances forcefully," implying that it is *on its way*, i.e., not yet here. In any event, there is no clear reference to the presence of the new order. This should be clear enough from the preceding praise of John as the greatest man then living. He would be surpassed only in the new age, which must not yet have arrived, since John is *still* the greatest (verse 11) as Jesus speaks.

Soon the reader of Matthew's gospel comes to another "present Kingdom" saying, or so it seems. Despite Ladd's exercising himself over the meaning of *ephthasen*,[3] Matthew 12:28 must, in context, be seen as implying nothing about the presence of the Kingdom. Rather, in view is imminent arrival in the future. This becomes evident from two important considerations. First, the exorcisms of Jesus are probably to be understood as the binding of the strong man *before* his house can be despoiled, i.e., *preparatory* to the eschatological overthrow of Satan.[4]

Secondly, Jesus says plainly in verse 32 that he and his accusers are yet in "this age," not "the age to come." This exact wording is Mat-

---

1 Hugh J. Schonfield, *The Authentic New Testament* (New York: New American Library, 1958), p. 104.

2 George Eldon Ladd, *The Presence of the Future: The Eschatology of Biblical Realism* (Grand Rapids: Eerdmans, 1974), p. 163.

3 Ibid., pp. 139-145.

4 Schweitzer, *Mystery of the Kingdom of God*, p. 98; see also Johannes Weiss, *Jesus' Proclamation of the Kingdom of God*. Trans. Richard Hyde Hiers and David Larrimore Holland. Lives of Jesus Series (Philadelphia: Fortress Press, 1971), pp. 42-43.

thew's contribution to his Markan source, so he must have understood the Kingdom (= age to come) as still future, though Mark's wording might not require this.

Similar preparatory work is in view with the various "sowing" images appearing in the chapter of Kingdom parables. Here, too, the Kingdom comes only after the consummation of the age (13:39, 40, 43).

In 21:28-32, doesn't Jesus speak of a present entering of whores and tax-collectors into the Kingdom? Again, one must read the text in the context of Matthew's general teaching. In 19:23; 18:3; 7:21-22, entrance into the Kingdom seems actually to take place in the future, though one may even now enter the door to the path toward the Kingdom (7:13-14). This is probably represented in shorthand fashion here, especially since the action of entering described here was a response to John's preaching (verse 32) which was, according to Matthew, purely futuristic. Also the parallel with 8:11-12 should be taken seriously. In both cases, the picture is of outcasts taking the place of the natural heirs of the Kingdom, and in chapter 8, the scene is explicitly a future one.

Similarly in 23:13-14, the rebuke need only imply that the Pharisees are refraining from doing what they must do to enter the Kingdom and that they prevent others as well.

Altogether, this brief survey indicates that, while some passages in Matthew might be understandable as teaching a presence of the Kingdom, they certainly neither have to be so interpreted nor are sufficient by themselves to substantiate the presence of such an idea in Matthew. Thus it is seriously dubious to interpret Matthew's Sermon on the Mount as presupposing such a thing.

What is the purpose of Jesus' teaching in Matthew, particularly the Sermon on the Mount? The framework of the book as a whole gives us our answer. Ethics in Matthew are the fruits of repentance for those who would escape the wrath to come. This is established at the beginning, in 3:8, 10, 12: "Turn or burn!" People must reform their lives while there is still time, or there will literally be hell to pay. The Sermon follows on the heels of this warning. It is an exposition of the fruit required (cf. 7:19). Again, the disciples are to go forth preaching the imminent end (10:7) presumably to get people to turn from sin and so escape the fate of Sodom and Gomorrah (10:15). The disciples are finally sent on their eleventh-hour mission of baptizing for repentance (28:19-20; cf, 24:14) like so many John the Baptists, teaching people to become disciples, i.e., to obey his commandments in preparation for the end.

Thus the Sermon is an interim-ethic (though this fact alone implies nothing about any limited validity of its demands). To put it another way, the Sermon sketches not the fruit that will be borne because one is already in the present Kingdom (Matthew knows of no such Kingdom), but rather the fruit that must be produced if one is ever to enter the future Kingdom. Schweitzer accurately describes "the *Leitmotiv* of the Sermon on the Mount" as this: "Nothing but the maintenance of the new morality in all relations of life guarantees entrance into the Kingdom."[1] This conclusion is amply reinforced by the content of the Sermon itself, to which attention must now be turned.

As already noted, the relation of the poor in spirit, the meek, the pure in heart, etc., to the Kingdom is a future one. (Only) people of this sort will inherit the eschatological blessings, so one had better be such a person. Things become even clearer with the rapid buildup of alternating promises and threats attached to various modes of conduct. If the disciple loses his distinctive tang, he will be thrown out and trampled (5:13; cf, John 15:6). If he keeps and teaches the Law he will be among the greatest when the Kingdom comes; otherwise he will be counted least of all (5:19). If you are not more righteous than the scribes and Pharisees (i.e., not hypocritical in your legal piety; see below), you will not enter the Kingdom. Anyone engendering anger, abuse, and strife will be remanded to the Judge and cast into hellfire (5:22, 25-26). Avoid acts of sin, or you will be thrown into Gehenna (5:29-30). The disciple will be God's child only if he loves his enemy (5:44-45). You will receive heavenly rewards if you endure persecution (5:11-12), greet enemies (5:46), give alms in secret (6:1-4), pray in secret (6:6), fast in secret (6:17-18), and shun earthly treasure (6:19-20). It will not do to spiritualize the notion of reward here. The point of Jesus' injunction seems to be that mere earthly admiration and money

---

1 Schweitzer, *Mystery of the Kingdom of God*, p. 98.

pale in comparison with the "pie in the sky" (cf, Rom. 8:10), so that one is only prudent[1] to cultivate genuine piety in order to qualify. (Of course, genuine piety rules out hypocritical religious observance that, in a mercenary spirit, seeks heavenly goodies for their own sake.[2] It is as if to say, "The only way to be rewarded is to do the act for its own sake, not for a reward, whether material or spiritual.").

One must forgive if he hopes to be forgiven (6:12, 14-15). Jeremias makes the mistake of reading in an idea of prior forgiveness which he derives from Matthew 18:23 ff, where the slave should have forgiven his fellow because the Master had already forgiven him. If Jeremias had heeded his own warning not to allegorize the parables,[3] he might have avoided this. The single point of the parable is the fate that lies in store for those who don't forgive. Similarly, one can escape God's judgment only if he refrains from judging others (7:1-2). If you do God's will you will survive the breaking of the storm of judgment (7:24-27).

The conditional nature of salvation could not be more clearly set forth. (Nor is it restricted to the Sermon itself; cf, e.g., Matt. 18:3; 19:17). Even if one chose, with Hunter and Jeremias, to presuppose membership in the Kingdom, the Sermon would by no stretch of the imagination leave the disciple's salvation a settled issue. In fact, however, the Sermon gives us a clear indication that nothing is presupposed. It contains clear exhortations to *begin* the life of discipleship,

---

1   "The Jesus of the Gospels appeals to each man's self-interest." Walter Kaufmann, *The Faith of a Heretic* (Garden City: Doubleday Anchor Books, 1963), pp. 211.

2   "I mean treasure is treasure, for heaven's sake. What's the difference whether the treasure is money, or property, or even culture, or even just plain knowledge? It all seemed like exactly the same thing to me, if you take off the wrapping—and it still does!" J.D. Salinger, *Franny and Zooey* (New York: Bantam Books, 1961).

3   Jeremias, *Sermon on the Mount*, pp. 26-27; Jeremias, *The Parables of Jesus*. Trans. S.H. Hooke. Scribner Studies in Biblical Interpretation (New York: Scribners, 1972), p. 67: "where reward and punishment were in question, there was a readiness... to seize on the allegorical interpretation."

to *start* the trek that will lead to salvation. Jesus' hearers must make the decision to seek the Kingdom instead of the commonplace pursuits in which they have always been engaged (6:33). They must yet *enter* the narrow gate that leads to life (7:13-14). In fact, the Sermon might properly be taken as an explicit answer to the question, "What must I do to inherit eternal life?"

When explicitly asked this question, Jesus said, "If you would enter life, keep the commandments" (19:17). Having suggested that the basic intention of the Sermon is "legalistic," this paper will now consider the role of legalism proper in Matthew's plan of salvation, especially in the Sermon on the Mount. The principle text is, of course, Matthew 5:17-19. How does Jesus "fulfill" the law? Does he set aside the letter of the Law by "filling it full" of the spirit of the Law? Does he set it aside by vicariously fulfilling its demands for us?[1] No, it is more likely that, whatever Jesus' original intent, Matthew understands him to mean fulfillment of Old Testament predictions, thus affirming the Law's (Scripture's) validity instead of destroying it. This is suggested by the frequent use of the word *pleroo* in the infancy narratives and a few places later in the book (1:22; 2:15, 17-18, 23; 4:14; 12:17; 13:14, 35; 21:4; 26:54, 56; 27:9). These fulfillments extend beyond the time of the giving of the Sermon into the time of the Passion, and apparently into the eschaton, since Jesus sees Danielic prophecy coming true then (24:15). Thus the reference "till heaven and earth pass away" is probably to be understood as literally guaranteeing the validity of the Law until the end of the world. This is clearly implied in 5:19, where one of the criteria for position in the Kingdom is how faithfully one has kept and taught the Law *until then*. The validity of the Law until the end is also indicated by the prediction that neglect of the Law (*anomia*, lawlessness) will be one of the signs of the end-time (24:12). Obviously, then, it must still be in force at that time.

How then are disciples to obey the Law? They must keep its provisions but with a whole heart. This is the difference between them and

---

1 Max Scheler, *Problems of a Sociology of Knowledge*. Trans. Manfred S. Frings. International Library of Sociology (London: Routledge & Kegan Paul, 1980), pp. 84-85.

the Pharisees, whose righteousness they are to surpass. That is, the Pharisees are right in what they say, they just don't live up to it (23:2-3), or so Matthew would have you believe; it is sectarian mudslinging. They are right to give alms, pray, and fast, but they are hypocritical about it, seeking only human admiration (6:1-6, 16-18). Their sin is not attachment to the Law; rather, it is that they are inwardly law*less* (23:28)! They have neglected weightier matters of the Law, but they were right to tithe herbs. In fact, this note (23:23) probably indicates that disciples should remember to do the same. Also, disciples are expected to keep the Sabbath until the end of the world (24:20). And though his understanding of clean and unclean is interiorized, Matthew wants to guard against actually abolishing kosher laws. This is indicated by his omission of Mark's comment, "Thus he declared all foods clean" (Mark 7:19; cf, Matt. 15:10-11). No wonder Matthew calls disciples "scribes trained for the Kingdom of Heaven." (13:52). "If you would enter life, keep the commandments" (19:17).

But Matthew plainly envisions some Christians not entering life because of their disregard for the law (7:21-23). They may have prophesied and performed exorcisms and miracles, but if they have not kept the Law, they will be repudiated. Whom does he have in mind? In order to grasp the *Sitz-im-Leben* of the book, one must recall what was said earlier about Matthew's concept of the apostolic mission. It is an offer of the gospel of the imminent Kingdom to the nations before the end of the age comes (cf, 24:14; 25:31 ff, where the nations are tried for their treatment of the Son of Man's "brethren," the missionaries sent to them; 28:19). Matthew's gospel, as is obvious from the ending, is self-consciously a response to Jesus' injunction to teach his commandments to the nations. Thus Matthew himself is contributing to the missionary effort. This is why he includes the long missionary discourse in chapter 10. It is to provide his missionaries with guidelines in the field.

His Jewish competitors and detractors lurk thinly veiled behind passages like 16:12; 23:15; 28:15 (cf, Acts 19:13 ff). Jesus' torah is contrasted with theirs in 11:28-30; 15:1-14; 16:6, 12. But these were not Matthew's only rivals. There were other Christian missionaries specializing in prophecy and miracle, but who disregarded the Law.

Matthew was not the only Jewish Christian incensed by such news (Acts 21:20-21). He was ready to deprive such workers of lawlessness of entrance into the Kingdom (7:21-23). Since they relaxed the commandments and taught others to do so, they would be least when the Kingdom arrived (5:19a). Matthew's missionaries, by contrast, were to assure themselves a high place in the Kingdom by faithful teaching of the Law (5:19b). Of course, others reversed the picture. Paul, who taught Gentiles to be free from the Law (Col. 2:16-17; Rom. 4:13-15; 1 Cor. 15:56; 2 Cor. 3:5-11; Gal. 2:15-21; 3:1-5, 10-14; 5:4, 18; 1 Tim. 1:8-11), as he himself was (1 Cor. 9:20), and cursed Jewish Christian missionaries who taught Gentile converts to obey the Law (Gal. 1:8-9; 6:12-13).

It is difficult to avoid the conclusion that Matthew's missionaries are just the kind Paul anathematized for preaching a gospel of Law (Gal. 1:8-9), and that Pauline missionaries advocating freedom from the Law are the very ones Matthew assigned the least place in the Kingdom of Heaven (5:19). Perhaps each attacked a misunderstood or caricatured position, but there does seem to be a real difference in perspective. And here, it is suggested, lies one root cause of the modern attempts to get around the legalistic character of the Sermon on the Mount. Is the Sermon law or gospel? Jeremias comes down on the side of "gospel" as he has defined it. But in so doing, he has missed the point of the Sermon. This is because he cannot see that for Matthew, gospel *is* Law.[1]

---

1 Not too long after writing this 1977 paper I stumbled upon Hans Windisch's great book *The Meaning of the Sermon on the Mount: A Contribution to the Historical Understanding of the Gospels and to the Problem of their True Exegesis*. Trans. S. MacLean Gilmour (Philadelphia: Westminster Press, 1951). Had I known of it I wouldn't have bothered to reinvent the wheel. "The religion of the Sermon on the Mount, like that of Judaism, is predominantly a religion of 'works' and of eschatological salvation ... The commands of the Sermon on the Mount are conditions of admittance to the Kingdom of Heaven ... Again and again it is plainly stated that only the person who has fulfilled the commands will withstand the judgment and be admitted to the Kingdom. The way to be saved is to do and to keep the commandments of Christ" (pp. 168-169). See what I mean?

[I wrote this paper for the sheer heck of it after reading A.M. Hunter's and Joachim Jeremias's books on the Sermon on the Mount. Then I asked Professor Bruce M. Metzger to read it and share any comments. Here's what he said. "This is a most interesting paper, well constructed and cogently argued. 'Almost thou persuadest me'! Zahn sees that Matthew writes for Jewish-Christians, and therefore expects that they will continue to be obedient to the Old Testament Law."]

Was There a Historical Apollonius of Tyana?

Apollonius of Tyana is a fascinating character in his own right, intrinsically deserving of scholarly attention. But much contemporary discussion of this ancient superhero is due to his possible relevance to the question of the historical Jesus, for his story as we read it in Philostratus' third-century hagiography *The Life of Apollonius of Tyana* bears a striking resemblance to that of the Christian Savior at many points. The parallels raise the question of literary genre, possible literary dependence, and euhemerism (whether a legendary superhero may be a magnification of an actual historical figure whose features may be dimly discerned via historical criticism). My focus is narrower still. It is sometimes observed that in Apollonius we have a strong precedent for Jesus as most scholars see him, as a genuine historical figure subsequently embellished by his admirers. After all, if we can discount the miracle stories attached to the sage of Tyana and still believe he existed, why not Jesus? Both figures conform in a whole host of details to the Mythic Hero Archetype,[1] but such figures may result from Man becoming Myth, or from Myth becoming Man. What are the deciding factors? And which was the case with our pair of subjects?

I shall suggest that all signs point to Apollonius having originated as a purely mythical hero, precisely like Asclepius, Hercules, Dionysus, and Theseus. Remember, these ancient heroes were also believed to have walked our earth in mortal form and to have worked wonders among the mortals whom they outwardly resembled. They were supposed to have been begotten upon mortal women by deities visiting from heavenly Olympus. When their earthly missions were complete,

---

1 Alan Dundes, Otto Rank, and Lord Raglan, *In Quest of the Hero*. Mythos: The Princeton/Bollingen Series in World Mythology (Princeton: Princeton University Press, 1990).

these demigods returned to heaven themselves. But they never in fact lived on earth. The only real difference between these ancient superheroes and Apollonius is that his (fictive) sojourn among mankind was imagined to have been more recent.

Philostratus informs us that he derived his biographical data on Apollonius from various sources including local legends/folk memories emanating from shrines boasting of visits from the philosopher-thaumaturge (much as tour guides cross their fingers behind their backs while telling visitors to Glastonbury that no less than Joseph of Arimathea, King Arthur, and Queen Guinevere lie buried there). But, he says, his principle source of information was the journal kept by Apollonius' disciple Damis the Assyrian, who carefully recorded every word and every movement of his master. But all this is a pose, a ruse, no more to be believed than Edgar Rice Burroughs when he claims his novel *A Princess of Mars* was recounted to him by Captain John Carter who had astrally traveled to the Red Planet. We do not believe, and of course are not intended to believe, that Carter actually encountered green-skinned, four-armed Tharks on Mars. Are we going to believe that Apollonius and company ran across dragons and humanoid giants? A narrative, as D.F. Strauss warned us, has no more credibility than the least believable parts of it.[1] And that pretty much poisons the well for Philostratus' hagiography of the man of Tyana.

But even if we did not have these fairy tale elements to contend with, we would still have to regard the whole work as fiction. There is simply no way Damis could have taken down Apollonius' discourses in such detail and with such eloquence unless the gods had provided him with a tape recorder. As we read, enthralled by the wit and wisdom of the philosopher, we find ourselves suspending disbelief. We look no deeper than the placid surface of the polished narrative, as when we watch a movie or read a novel (which is what we are doing here). It is possible that Philostratus was working from a set of notes taken down by Damis, but what reason is there to think so? Occam's Razor warns

---

1 David Friedrich Strauss, *The Life of Jesus Critically Examined.* Trans. George Eliot (Mary Ann Evans). Lives of Jesus Series (Philadelphia: Fortress Press, 1972), pp. 90-91.

us not to posit redundant and superfluous explanations. If it reads like a work of *de novo* fiction, why should we complicate things by positing extra ostensible causes for the effect, which do nothing to make the work more understandable? So fiction it is.

But why the pose that Apollonius was a figure of recent history? Apollonius supposedly lived in the first century CE. Philostratus was writing about him in the third. Others had written of Apollonius, e.g., Moeragenes, whose account did not meet with Philostratus' approval. But does the fact that this character, *as* a character, already existed establish his existence as a historical figure? It only proves that Philostratus was not his inventor..

More simply, it is by no means unlikely that Philostratus and Moeragenes were alike simply taking for granted the result of the process of "euhemerizing" an ancient, mythic hero, distilling a whittled-down, hypothetically historical prototype, just as euhemerists like Herodotus posited a historical Hercules, an ancient Steve Reeves.

Perhaps the strongest argument for a historical Apollonius has been what New Testament scholars like to call the criterion of embarrassment: does a text retain what looks like a loose end, a clue that the story once read differently? Is a text trying to refute a previous understanding that clashes with the author's preferred version? Scholars point to Mark's story of John baptizing Jesus as one of these. The very idea of Jesus needing the ministrations of John proved an embarrassment to subsequent Christians, and so the other gospels rewrite the scene to make it theologically palatable. Who would have made up such a story? Thus, apologists argue that Jesus' baptism must actually have taken place. But I have argued that this reasoning is fatally flawed. The contrast need not be between original events and later belief. It is just as likely that the embarrassment to later belief is merely *an earlier form of belief.* That is, perhaps Mark saw nothing amiss in his account of the Jordan baptism, which he may have intended as an example for Christian readers to follow.[1] And as such the story might have been Mark's invention, not history at all.

---

1 Charles Guignebert, *Jesus.* Trans. S.H. Hooke (New Hyde Park: University Books, 1956), pp. 147-148.

In the case of Apollonius, scholars have reasoned that, if Philostratus felt he had to clean up his hero's reputation, making him a sublime philosopher instead of a charlatan conjurer, wouldn't that imply that Apollonius actually *was* a magician? Why would he invent such a strike against Apollonius? But this fails, too. It seems rather that Philostratus was trying to rebut a general disdain of philosophy and philosophers by those who considered them no more than frauds and parasites, just as we read in the Apocryphal Acts of the Apostles how pagan authorities, baffled at the Encratite celibacy gospel, had its preachers, Paul, Thomas, et. al., arrested as trouble-making wizards.

> Nero was opposed to philosophy, because he suspected its devotees to be addicted to magic, and of being diviners in disguise; and at last the philosopher's mantle brought its wearers before the law courts, as if it were a mere cloak of the divining art. I will not mention other names, but Musonius of Babylon, a man only second to Apollonius, was thrown into prison for the crime of being a sage, and there lay in danger of death; and he would have died for all his gaoler cared, if it had not been for the strength of his constitution. (4:35)[1]

I want to start with a form-critical analysis of the miracle stories starring Apollonius in order to determine, if possible, where they came from and what purpose they served. Do they seem to presuppose or imply an origin in a genuine historical figure or only the evolution of a mythic character like Hercules or Asclepius? And what light do they shed on claims for an eyewitness origin of the narratives?

NATIVITY STORIES

> To his mother, just before [Apollonius] was born, there came an apparition of Proteus, who changes his form so much in Homer, in the guise of an Egyptian demon. She was in no way frightened but asked what sort of child she would bear. And he answered, "Myself." "And who are you?" she asked. "Proteus," he answered, "the god of Egypt." (1:4)

---

1 I am using the F.C. Conybeare translation.

Does this open the possibility that Apollonius is a fictive historicization of the mythical Proteus? Obviously, this annunciation tale is mythical. No one disputes that. The real question is whether the larger Apollonius narrative of which it forms a tiny part, is of any different character. In one sense, it is, insofar as the Apollonius epic is made the vehicle for huge amounts of philosophical paraenesis aimed (where else?) at the readers for their edification. Apollonius becomes the mouthpiece for Philostratus himself, just as Socrates was for Plato. This becomes blatantly obvious when it comes to the trial of Apollonius. The sage is called before the fiendish emperor Domitian. There is an exchange, but then Apollonius abruptly and literally vanishes into thin air, to reappear across the Mediterranean to the speechless astonishment of his disciples, whom he had sent on ahead. But then Philostratus shares with us the speech Apollonius *would* have given had he not so rudely departed. Wait a minute! Which is it? Philostratus has already made it clear (in a passage to be considered presently) that Apollonius planned to teleport away from the courtroom, as he did, so he could not have prepared the speech Philostratus shares with us. And was Apollonius planning to *read* the speech? And how would Philostratus have obtained a copy? He thus reveals himself as the omniscient narrator using his hero as a ventriloquist dummy.

As for the actual "events" of Apollonius' life, is any of them free from strong suspicion of being entirely fictive and fanciful? I think that the sage of Tyana is here revealed as fully mythical as the shape-shifting god Proteus of whom he is the avatar. Traditionally we have supposed these fanciful episodes and anecdotes were merely decorative embellishments to highlight the greatness of his hero for the edification of his original audiences. But if the whole thing looks like a myth-cycle, why should we suppose it rests upon any (in any case indiscernible) historical basis? Let William of Occam again be our conscience: the notion of a more modest, historical Apollonius is a fifth wheel, a redundant and superfluous pseudo-explanation.

One more note: Proteus, like various ancient gods, could assume any form at will, which means he had no true form at all, but only *seemed* to be this or that. Thus Proteus' announcement of his own impending birth as Apollonius means that the birth itself was a holy sham, as is pretty much made explicit in this passage. My point, here as elsewhere, is that Philostratus is actually presenting his hero as a theophany, not as a wise mortal later rewarded by exaltation to heaven.

The Life of Apollonius of Tyana begins (and continues) by extolling Apollonius as superior to all rivals. But eventually we are surprised to see our author lionizing someone else. When Apollonius betakes himself to India, he gladly defers to the venerable Gymnosophists, or naked philosophers,[1] as wiser than himself. He does not presume to teach them aught, but rejoices to sit under their instruction. Apollonius almost becomes a John the Baptist glorifying a greater: "The friend of the bridegroom, who stands and hears him, rejoices greatly at the bridegroom's voice; therefore this joy of mine is now full. He must increase, but I must decrease." (John 3:29b-30). It would appear that Philostratus himself greatly admired what he knew of Indian philosophy and used his commission to eulogize Apollonius[2] as an opportunity to promote exotic Oriental mysticism to his Hellenistic readership.

This may account for the similarities between the annunciation to Apollonius' mother and annunciation/nativity stories of the Buddha. First, here is Apollonius' birth story.

> Now he is said to have been born in a meadow... [J]ust as the hour of his birth was approaching, his mother was warned in a dream to walk out into the meadow and pluck the flowers; and in due course she came there and her maids attended to the flowers, scattering themselves over the meadow, while she fell asleep lying on the grass. Thereupon the swans who fed in the meadow set up a dance around her as she slept, and lifting their wings, as they are wont to do, cried out aloud all at once, for there was somewhat of a breeze blowing in the meadow. She then leaped up at the sound of their song and bore her child, for any sudden fright is apt

---

1 The Jainists are divided, still today, between the Digambara ("sky-clad," i.e., naked) faction and the Svetambara ("white-clad," i.e., loincloth-wearers) sects.

2 The Empress Julia Domna hired him to write it.

to bring on a premature delivery. But the people of that country say that just at the moment of the birth, a thunderbolt seemed about to fall to earth and then rose up into the air and disappeared aloft; and the gods thereby indicated, I think, the great distinction to which the sage was to attain, and hinted in advance how he would transcend all things upon earth and approach the gods. (1:4-5)

Now, two versions of the Buddha's annunciation and birth:

Before she conceived, she saw in her sleep a white lord of elephants entering her body, yet she felt thereby no pain. [...] In that glorious grove the queen perceived that the time of her delivery was at hand. Then... from the side of the queen... a son was born for the weal of the world, without her suffering either pain or illness. [...] When in due course he had issued from the womb, he appeared as if he had descended from the sky, for he did not come into the world through the portal of life; and, since he had purified his being through many aeons, he was born not ignorant but fully conscious. (*Buddhacarita*, i. 4, 8, 9, 11)[1]

Bodhisattva, the foremost in three worlds, worshipped by the world, seeing the (right) season, freed himself from the wonderful Tusita abode[2] ... and... became a baby white elephant with six tusks... the set of tusks made of gold... and entered on the right side, the womb of his mother... Mayadevi, sleeping on a comfortable bed, had this dream: "A lordly elephant the colour of snow or silver, with six tusks... entered my womb." [...] Then Mayadevi... arose from her beautiful bed... descended from the top of the magnificent palace, going into the *asoka* grove, seated [herself] comfortably in the *asoka* grove. [...] Then Mayadevi, entering the Lumbini Park..., walked from tree to tree... until she came gradually to that *plaska* tree, the greatest and most excellent jewel of trees... Then that *plaska* tree, bent by Bodhisattva's glory, bowed down. Then Mayadevi stretched out her right arm like the lightning in the sky...

---

1 *The Buddhacarita, or Acts of the Buddha*. Trans. E.H. Johnston (Delhi: Motilal Banarsidass Publishers, 1992), pp. 2-3.

2 One of the Buddhist heavens.

Magically arriving in this fashion, Bodhisattva remained in his mother's womb. At the completion of ten months he issued from the right side of his mother. (*Lalitavistara*, VI. 2, 3, 22; VII.22)[1]

You can see that both Buddhist Nativity stories make clear that the infant to be born (in a purely illusory manner) *is* an illusion, only outwardly a baby, as he merely uses a woman's womb as a conduit. He is a pre-existent heavenly being, already filled with supernatural wisdom. Furthermore, both the Buddha's mother and Apollonius' mother give birth in a peaceful rustic location, and both births are signaled by either a lightning bolt or a gesture reminiscent of one. It wouldn't surprise me if the Apollonius Nativity has been influenced by its Buddhist counterpart. And of course both are not only equally mythical, but they are part of completely mythical epics. If there was a historical Gautama Buddha, as most assume, whoever and whatever he may have been, he cannot be found in the canonical hagiographies. I side with older scholars who discounted any historical existence of the Buddha. Asian Buddhists (the real thing) by and large take umbrage at the suggestion of Western Indologists that the twenty-four previous Buddhas posited by Buddhist mythology were not in fact real individuals, but rather fictive retrojections of the one historical Buddha. All of them, says the doctrine, lived the same life, the same pattern identically, one after another, the familiar story of the Buddha's Nativity, the Four Passing Sights, the Great Renunciation, sitting in the shade of the Bodhi Tree, etc. Western scholars hold that this pattern began with Gautama and was then generalized in order to render Buddhism cyclical throughout eternity. Eastern Buddhists insist the twenty-five Bud-

---

1 *The Lalitavistara*. Trans. Bijoya Goswami. Bibliotheca Indica Series No. 320 (Kolkata: The Asiatic Society, 2001), pp. 61, 83, 84. Also see Edward J. Thomas, *The Life of Buddha as History and Legend*. The History of Civilizations (London: Routledge & Kegan Paul, 1949), Chapter III, "The Birth of Buddha," pp. 27-37; H.W. Schumann, *The Historical Buddha: The Times, Life and Teachings of the Founder of Buddhism*. Trans. M. O'C. Walshe (London: The Penguin Group, 1989), Chapter 1, "Youth, Quest and Enlightenment," section 2, "Siddhattha's origins and birth," pp. 6-9.

dhas are all equally historical. And I think they are right in that they all stand or fall together. I think the pattern is entirely mythical, and that Western scholars are just trying to refashion an Eastern religion in the image of a Western "revealed religion" with a historical founder.

Why do I belabor this? My ultimate goal is to disarm the Jesus-historicist argument that, despite the mythical encrustations, Jesus could still have been as (remotely) historical as Apollonius, likewise a historical figure buried beneath six feet of legend. I am arguing that there may well have been no historical Apollonius either. And, lest someone think to defend Apollonius' historical reality by comparing him to a probably historical Buddha clad in a Technicolor Dream Coat of pious fantasy, I mean to cut off such a strategy by suggesting the Buddha is in exactly the same historiographical predicament.

DOCTOR SHOPPING

The Hellenistic world witnessed an unprecedented variety of competing cults and sects. Luckily, this competition was largely non-violent. But precisely this tolerant atmosphere occasioned stiffer competition, since it created a free market. Religions advertized, as attested by the inscribed healing testimonies mounted on the walls of the Epidaurus shrine of Asclepius. These (outlandish) healing miracles were, let's face it, commercials. A popular kind of commercial today compares and contrasts the sponsor's product with its rival, "Brand X." Which one does a better job of cleansing your sink? But these ads are nothing new. John's gospel contains at least two of them. John 3:25-30, already mentioned, juxtaposes John's baptismal ministry with Jesus' (i.e., Christian baptism), at the expense of the former. Two chapters later we witness the superiority of Jesus as a healer to the famous shrine of Bethsaida with its fatal design flaw (John 5:7). Mark 5:25-34 stresses the superiority of Jesus, who can literally heal the sick without even trying, to conventional medicine which has bankrupted the bleeding woman with no results. "Who ya gonna call?" We have a similar commercial on behalf of our Apollonius.

> An Assyrian stripling came to [the temple of] Asclepius, and though he was sick, yet he lived the life of luxury... and finding his pleasure in

drunkenness took no care to dry up his malady. On this account then Asclepius took no care of him, and did not visit him even in a dream. The youth grumbled at this, and thereupon the god, standing over him, said, "If you were to consult Apollonius you would be easier." He therefore went to Apollonius, and said: "What is there in your wisdom that I can profit by? for Asclepius bids me consult you." And he replied: "I can advise you of what, under the circumstances, will be most valuable to you; for I suppose you want to get well." "Yes, by Zeus," answered the other, "I want the health which Asclepius promises, but never gives." "Hush," said the other, "for he gives to those who desire it, but you do things that irritate and aggravate your disease, for you give yourself up to luxury, and you accumulate delicate viands upon your water-logged and worn-out stomach, and as it were, choke water with a flood of mud." (1:9)

Apollonius is doing his residency at the temple of Asclepius, the healing god. Asclepius is stumped: he cannot help this young epicure, so he refers him to Apollonius. Interestingly, the key to his recovery is the same one Jesus uses at the Pool of Bethesda: "Do you *want* to be healed?" (John 5:6). Apollonius trumps Asclepius. Asclepius thus becomes a John the Baptist for Apollonius' Jesus. But there is something else here: at first it looks as if we have a contrast between a celestial god and a wise man on earth. But remember who Asclepius was. He was a completely mythical character, a demigod fathered upon the mortal Coronis by the god Apollo. He had adventures on earth among mortals. This lasted until Asclepius crossed the line by raising someone from the dead. Zeus struck down Asclepius for his hubris but then raptured him to heaven, where he continued to live as a god. Henceforth he would appear to seekers in dreams as they passed the night in local Asclepiums (his healing shines), either healing them on the spot or else prescribing some treatment (or weird stunt) that was supposed to effect the desired cure. There never was a mortal, historical Asclepius (as all admit). His earthly career is simply part of his myth cycle that provided the "back story," the rationale, for the Asclepium franchise. I'm thinking that the career of Apollonius has the same origin and function. Just as the ancients believed Asclepius was a historical character, taking the myth literally, I think the "historical Apollonius" was cut from the same cloth.

RAISING THE DEAD

Probably the best known Apollonius miracle story fits neatly into another category: the rescue from premature burial. Jesus' raising of the Nain widow's son (Luke 7:11-11-17), of Jairus' daughter (Mark 5:21-24a, 35-43), and even the "resurrection" of Lazarus (John chapter 11) are of this type. We find others in *The Story of Apollonius, King of Tyre* and in Lucius Apuleius's *The Golden Ass*. The stories presuppose the widespread occurrence of premature burials in antiquity, when it was more difficult to distinguish deep coma from real death. The matter was frequently treated in medical texts of the time.[1] It is not unlikely that this story is a cautionary tale, urging physicians to imagine the needless tragedies that might stem from their carelessness. Philostratus almost indicates as much when, at the close of the episode, he suggests Apollonius' feat might be the result of medical acumen rather than divine power.

> Here too is a miracle which Apollonius worked: A girl had died just in the hour of her marriage, and the bridegroom was following her bier lamenting as was natural his marriage left unfulfilled, and the whole of Rome was mourning with him, for the maiden belonged to a consular family. Apollonius then witnessing their grief, said: "Put down the bier, for I will stay the tears that you are shedding for this maiden." And withal he asked what was her name. The crowd accordingly thought he was about to deliver such an oration as is commonly delivered as much to grace the funeral as to stir up lamentation; but he did nothing of the kind, but merely touching her and whispering in secret some spell over her, at once woke up the maiden from her seeming death; and the girl spoke out loud, and returned to her father's house, just as Alcestis did when she was brought back to life by Hercules.
>
> And the relations of the maiden wanted to present him with the sum of 150,000 sesterces, but he said that he would freely present the money

---

1   J. Duncan M. Derrett, *The Anastasis: The Resurrection of Jesus as an Historical Event* (Shipston-on-Stour: Peter Drinkwater, 1982), Chapter III, "Anastasis in the Ancient World," pp. 19-27.

to the young lady by way of a dowry. Now whether he detected some spark of life in her [obviously Philostratus' preferred theory, given the above reference to "seeming death"], which those who were nursing her had not noticed, - for it is said that although it was raining at the time, a vapour went up from her face - or whether life was really extinct, and he restored it by the warmth of his touch, is a mysterious problem which neither I myself nor those who were present could decide. (4:45)

We must not be too quick to pass by the parallel Philostratus draws between Apollonius and Hercules. Essentially, Apollonius simply repeats Hercules' feat of resurrection. I wonder if this is not because Philostratus has simply borrowed the original Hercules story and loaned it to his hero Apollonius. This speculation may gain substance from our consideration of another story immediately below.

EXORCISMS

When the plague began to rage in Ephesus, and no remedy sufficed to check it, they sent a deputation to Apollonius, asking him to become physician of their infirmity; and he thought that he ought not to postpone his journey, but said, "Let us go." And forthwith he was in Ephesus... He therefore called together the Ephesians, and said: "Take courage, for I will to-day put a stop to the course of the disease." And with these words he led the population entire to the theatre, where the image of the Averting god has [since] been set up. And there he saw what seemed an old mendicant artfully blinking his eyes as if blind, and he carried a wallet and a crust of bread in it; and he was clad in rags and was very squalid of countenance. Apollonius therefore ranged the Ephesians around him and said: "Pick up as many stones as you can and hurl them at this enemy of the gods." Now the Ephesians wondered what he meant, and were shocked at the idea of murdering a stranger so manifestly miserable; for he was begging and praying them to take mercy upon him. Nevertheless Apollonius insisted and egged on the Ephesians to launch themselves on him and not let him go. And as soon as some of them began to take shots and hit him with their stones, the beggar who had seemed to blink and be blind, gave them all a sudden glance and showed that his eyes were full of fire. Then the Ephesians recognised that he was a demon, and they stoned him so thoroughly that their stones were heaped into a great cairn around him. After a little pause Apollonius bade them remove the stones and acquaint themselves with the wild animal they had slain. When therefore they had exposed the object they thought they had thrown their missiles at, they found that he had disappeared and instead of him there was found a hound who resembled in form and look a Molossian dog, but was in size the equal of the largest lion; there he lay before their eyes, pounded to a pulp by their stones and vomiting foam as mad dogs do. Accordingly the statue of the Averting god, namely Hercules, has been set up over the spot where the ghost was slain. (5:10)

Again, is Apollonius Hercules? Otherwise, why not a statue of Apollonius who according to the present narrative, "averted" the plague?[1] I think here of Martin Noth's *redundancy principle*. In his scrutiny of the Moses stories in the Pentateuch,[2] Noth asks why some of the tales feature various characters who have no appreciable reason for crowding the stage. Why do the superfluous Nadab and Abihu get to accompany Moses and Aaron to the mountaintop to behold the God of Israel (Exod. 24:9-10). They have no contribution to make. Again, what is Moses doing passively standing by as Aaron performs this or that miracle before Pharaoh? The answer Noth offers is quite simple as well as perfectly cogent: originally the mountaintop epiphany starred *only* Nadab and Abihu, who had formerly been important characters in Jewish lore. Once their stock had fallen and that of Moses had risen, the central role was transferred to him. Something quite similar occurs

---

1　In his account of Apollonius' apologia, which the sage never got to deliver, Philostratus has Apollonius say he himself caused the statue of Hercules to be erected in Ephesus, but this sequence reinterprets various earlier episodes, indicating the version in the speech is a redactional rewrite and reinterpretation of the original story. We need not go back to the Ephesus exorcism and read the apologia version into it.

2　Martin Noth, *A History of Pentateuchal Traditions*. Trans. Bernhard W. Anderson (Englewood Cliffs: Prentice-Hall, 1972), pp 186-187.

when we compare 1 Samuel 17:41-49 with 2 Samuel 21:19. In 2 Samuel we read that the Philistine giant Goliath was slain by the once-celebrated hero Elhanan. But 1 Samuel credits the same deed to the later, more popular hero David. David was not shoe-honed into Elhanan's story, elbowing Elhanan aside but retaining him on the sideline. Both versions were preserved, though separated by a considerable mass of buffer text. But it was the same "redundancy" phenomenon. Similarly, originally it was Moses who wrought all the miracles in the presence of Pharaoh. Aaron had nothing to do with it, until, that is, the priestly faction, for whom Aaron served as figurehead, got their hands on the stories and pretty much replaced Moses with their favorite, Aaron, though they dared not omit Moses altogether. I am suggesting that, in the very same way, the tell-tale mention of Hercules the Averter implies his original role as the one that stymied the Ephesian plague. Philostratus has replaced Hercules with an equally mythical Apollonius.

Remember that, just like Asclepius, Hercules was regarded as a historical individual, albeit a demigod, son of Zeus. He was believed to have lived on earth among men and was finally resurrected and assumed into heaven. Just like Apollonius. Again, I think that Apollonius' earthly career was just as mythical, only the credulous belief in his historical existence for some reason outlasted that of his mythical colleagues.

But there is yet another layer to this exorcism story. It is really, at bottom, a *scapegoat* legend as described by Rene Girard.[1] Such tales, he explains, reflect the ancient means of dealing with major crises, sacrificial crises. Briefly, here is the theory. Society (or a sub-society within it) breaks down, violence erupting between two classes, castes, factions, whatever. Social order disintegrates or is nearly at that point. This condition is recognized as worse than whatever had occasioned the tumult. Both sides seek resolution, but each is equally red-handed, both having partaken of the rampant violence. It no longer matters who started it or why. Neither side will admit (or can remember if) they were the one to start it. So, to get beyond this impasse, they zero in on

---

1 René Girard, *Violence and the Sacred*. Trans. Patrick Gregory (Baltimore: Johns Hopkins University Press, 1977), pp. 12-13, 64-65.

some socially marginal figure belonging to neither faction, perhaps a foreigner in their midst. Or they finger a culprit from one side or the other by flipping the oracular coin. All ascribe blame to this poor bastard, who is now imagined to be a sorcerer or demon who cast the apple of discord. If they eliminate him, all should return to normal. The execution is carried out, if possible, without anyone physically touching victim lest the executioner be infected with the uncleanness of the culprit. It may be that no single executioner does the job; everyone must participate so that it is a communal act and no one individual can be specified by the victim's loved ones as a target of escalating vendetta (cf., the execution of Achan by communal stoning in Joshua 7:24-26).

Henceforth, this scapegoat gets transformed into a savior figure by virtue of his once-insidious power now having restored peace. The violence that had raged with terrible results is henceforth channeled by means of ritual sacrifice, usually of animals. These sacrifices remind the people of the violence now happily suppressed and again put under control: is too terrible ever to be let out of the bottle again.

This system is effective even when the people no longer consciously recall (in subsequent generations) the original (and originary) violence; in fact such amnesia is crucial to the system of keeping the lid on. But suppose the culture loses faith in the efficacy of the ritual sacrifices required of them or enacted on their behalf by the authorities? This may happen because the priestly authorities lose credibility or the worshippers become alienated from the animal sacrifices, e.g., because they no longer offer an animal of their own but pay for one on-site. Then the aqueducts of violence shatter and the once-channeled savagery may break out anew.

I just noted the role of suppression and community amnesia. Like a repressed trauma in an individual peeking out of the subconscious in the forms of dreams, hysterical conversion symptoms, and Freudian slips, so the originary violence, the social chaos, lingers in the form of myth, in which everything is superficially transformed. To wit, the two factions become narrative characters, specifically "mimetic twins," "monstrous doubles." These may be biological siblings (Cain and Abel, Romulus and Remus) or simply similar characters set against one another. The "war of all against all," a plague of spreading violence, may be represented as a spreading disease plague.

The Ephesus episode, not exactly an exorcism, is a near-perfect example of the Girardian scapegoat myth. The plague, as in the Oedipus cycle, is represented as a disease outbreak but may conceal originally physical strife. Between whom? Well, who are the rival twins in the Apollonius story? They are, of course, Apollonius himself and the vagabond beggar, who bears a suspicious resemblance to your typical Cynic philosopher: an itinerant beggar carrying a pouch/purse in which to store the day's receipts, like the begging bowl of the Buddhist mendicant. Ordinarily we do not envision strife between (Neo-)Pythagoreans like Apollonius and the Cynics, but it is not impossible. What might have been the issue? This gets a bit foggy, but there is certainly a "Girardian" clue here. Remember that the decay of sacrifice is integral to the crisis, as the sacred "safety valve" of social violence is rendered nonfunctional. What do we know about the Cynics and Apollonius with regard to sacrifice"? The Cynics utterly rejected such mummery, as they viewed it. One's only "religious" duty was to live in accordance with nature by reason, shunning all traditional social convention. What relevance might the Cynic position on sacrifice have on social breakdown? Simply that, if sacrifice kept violence under control, its abolition would sooner or later unleash the beast.

How about the stance of Apollonius? He revered sacrifice but insisted that no animal blood be shed. Naturally, there had always been other options: wave offerings, poured-out drink offerings, etc. Doing away with meat-sacrifice would, obviously, strike many as an evisceration of the sacrificial system (if you'll forgive the pun). Insofar as one counted on animal sacrifice to avert divine wrath, one must have been pretty alarmed at the prospect of putting the gods on an all-vegetarian diet.[1] Here we have all the ingredients of a sacrificial crisis. That this scenario possesses at least narrative verisimilitude is evident from a couple of other ancient texts. In Acts 19:23-41, Paul's men manage narrowly to avoid a bloody riot (in *Ephesus* of all places!), with Arte-

---

1 I suspect the gods' reaction would be about like mine. Pass me that pot roast, will you?

mis worshippers targeting Christians and Jews. The issue is both theological and economical in that these particular devotees of the many-breasted goddess happen to be traders in religious souvenirs who fear the loss of income if the Christian preachers succeed in siphoning off worshippers of Artemis. And in Pliny's famous letter to Trajan, Pliny expresses his concern that the local meat markets are losing business because people are abandoning the pagan gods for Christ, hence no sacrifices. The result? Violent persecution. Another sacrificial crisis leading to bloodshed.

What exactly is the function of Apollonius' ratting out the vagrant as a "devil in disguise"?[1] On the story level, of course, the point is to showcase Apollonius' preternatural sensitivity: he sees through the demon's human disguise where others do not and cannot. But the subtext shows us the designation of a socially marginal scapegoat, a man with no family or allies to take vengeance against his executioners, which would only reignite the very cycle of violence the designation of a scapegoat is designed to quell. The significance of Apollonius selecting this pariah is the same: the selection being made via supernatural knowledge removes the one who does the selecting from the danger of reprisals: after all, he was just a channel for the word of god. To punish him must call down the wrath of Nemesis upon oneself. And when Apollonius bids the crowd to stone the victim, he is following the scapegoating tradition of laying no one's hand on the culprit, yet making everyone share in the execution.

As Apollonius, Damis, and the Cowardly Lion head east, they encounter various oddities as one should expect in such exotic regions of the imagination.

Having passed the Caucasus our travelers say they saw men four cubits height, and they were already black, and that when they passed over the river Indus they saw others five cubits in height. But on their way to this river our wayfarers found the following incidents worthy of notice. For they were traveling by bright moonlight, when the figure of an *empusa* or hobgoblin appeared to them, that changed from one form into another,

---

1 "Oh yes you are!"

and sometimes vanished into nothing. And Apollonius realized what it was, and himself heaped abuse on the hobgoblin and instructed his party to do the same, saying that this was the right remedy for such a visitation. And the phantasm fled away shrieking even as ghosts do. (2:4)

Is this an exorcism paradigm, a "how-to" guide for dispatching malevolent spooks? In a sense, yes, once you recall Martin Luther's dictum, "The devil, proud spirit, cannot endure to be mocked." The best technique to deal with superstitious fears is laughing them off.

We have to do with a genuine exorcism in the following passage from *The Life of Apollonius of Tyana*, though, quite surprisingly, it is not performed by Apollonius! The scene is reminiscent of Gurdjieff's *Meetings with Remarkable Men*. It is set in the Mystic East, with Apollonius soaking up the enlightened wisdom of the naked masters.

This discussion was interrupted by the appearance among the sages of the messenger bringing in certain Indians who were in want of succor. And he brought forward a poor woman who interceded in behalf of her child, who was, she said, a boy of sixteen years of age, but had been for two years possessed by a devil. Now the character of the devil was that of a mocker and a liar. Here one of the sages asked, why she said this, and she replied: "This child of mine is extremely good-looking, and therefore the devil is amorous of him and will not allow him to retain his reason, nor will he permit him to go to school, or to learn archery, nor even to remain at home, but drives him out into desert places. And the boy does not even retain his own voice, but speaks in a deep hollow tone, as men do; and he looks at you with other eyes rather than with his own. As for myself I weep over all this and I tear my cheeks, and I rebuke my son so far as I well may; but he does not know me. And I made my mind to repair hither, indeed I planned to do so a year ago; only the demon discovered himself using my child as a mask, and what he told me was this, that he was the ghost of a man, who fell long ago in battle, but that at death he was passionately attached to his wife. Now he had been dead for only three days when his wife insulted their union by marrying another man, and the consequence was that he had come to detest the love of women, and had transferred himself wholly into this boy. But he promised, if I would only not denounce him to yourselves, to endow the child with many noble blessings. As for myself, I was influenced by these promises; but he has put me off and off for such a long time now, that he has got sole control of my household, yet has no honest or true intentions." Here the sage [Iarchus] asked afresh, if the boy was at hand; and she said not, for, although she had done all she could to get him to come with her, the demon had threatened her with steep places and precipices and declared that he would kill her son, "in case," she added, "I haled him hither for trial." "Take courage," said the sage, "for he will not slay him when he has read this." And so saying he drew a letter out of his bosom and gave it to the woman; and the letter, it appears, was addressed to the ghost and contained threats of an alarming kind. (3:38)

I venture to suggest that, in effect, the contents of the potent letter are the contents of this very story. The writ of exorcism is the story in which it appears. The story was written to be read aloud as an exorcistic formula. Origen tells us that in his day certain gospel stories were read for precisely this purpose.[1] Stories of Elijah's defeat of demons were so used by Jewish exorcists in the Middle Ages.[2] It looks like Mark already designed certain healing and exorcism stories with such use in mind, as when he retained Jesus' words in Aramaic, *Ephphatha* ("be opened") in Mark 7:34 and *Talitha cumi* ("Little girl, get up!") in Mark 5:41 on the assumption that what Jesus had said in such cases would be the best magic formula when Christian healers sought to repeat his feats. This is almost explicit in the story of the deaf-mute epileptic which admits an exorcism might not work immediately, requiring perhaps a preliminary regimen of prayer or, in particularly difficult cases, fasting, too (Mark 9:29, some manuscripts of which add "and fasting").

The exorcism is twice removed from Apollonius, being effected via a letter at a distance, and that by Iarchus, not Apollonius. Think

---

1 Stevan L. Davies, *The Revolt of the Widows: The Social World of the Apocryphal Acts* (Carbondale: Southern Illinois University Press, 1980), pp. 21-27.

2 Raphael Patai, *The Hebrew Goddess* (New York: Avon/Discus Books, 1978), pp. 187-189.

of the distance healings in the gospels, where Jesus heals the child (Mark 7:24-30) or servant (Luke 7:1-10) of a Gentile. The point is to legitimate the early church's mission to Gentiles, initially quite controversial among staunch Jewish Christians (see Acts chapters 11-12, 15). Jesus is shown healing *the next generation* and Gentiles at that. In other words, though the Gentile Mission is pictured as commencing after the departure of Jesus, these stories retroject Jesus' approval of it into the time of Jesus. I see the double-distancing of this exorcism from Apollonius as having the same function: it claims Apollonius' endorsement of what a later disciple (Philostratus) favors. Furthermore, Philostratus makes the Gymnosophists as much superior to Apollonius as he made Apollonius superior to Asclepius. Apollonius is used here to endorse the wisdom of India, which is available to Philostratus' readers through *written documents*, symbolized by this exorcistic letter.

The next two exorcism stories seem to me to be Philostratus' parables teaching the powerful utility of philosophy for combating the dangerous lusts of the flesh.

Now while he was discussing the question of libations, there chanced to be present in his audience a young dandy who bore so evil a reputation for licentiousness that his conduct had long been the subject of coarse street-corner songs. His home was Corcyra, and he traced his pedigree to Alcinous the Phaeacian who entertained Odysseus. Apollonius then was talking about libations, and was urging them not to drink out of a particular cup, but to reserve it for the gods, without ever touching it or drinking out of it. But when he also urged them to have handles on the cup, and to pour the libation over the handle, because that is the part at which men are least likely to drink, the youth burst out into loud and coarse laughter, and quite drowned his voice. Then Apollonius looked up and said: "It is not yourself that perpetrates this insult, but the demon, who drives you without your knowing it." And in fact the youth was, without knowing it, possessed by a devil; for he would laugh at things that no one else laughed at, and then would fall to weeping for no reason at all, and he would talk and sing to himself. Now most people thought that it was boisterous humor of youth which led him into excesses; but he was really the mouthpiece of a devil, though it only seemed a drunken frolic in which on that occasion he was indulging. Now, when Apollonius gazed on him, the ghost in him began to utter cries of fear and rage, such as one hears from people who are being branded or racked; and the ghost swore that he would leave the young man alone and never take possession of any man again. But Apollonius addressed him with anger, as a master might a shifty, rascally, and shameless slave and so on, and he ordered him to quit the young man and show by a visible sign that he had done so. "I will throw down yonder statue," said the devil, and pointed to one of the images which were there in the king's portico, for there it was that the scene took place. But when the statue began by moving gently, and then fell down, it would defy anyone to describe the hubbub which arose thereat and the way they clapped their hands with wonder. But the young man rubbed his eyes as if he had just woke up, and he looked towards the rays of the sun, and assumed a modest aspect, as all had their attention concentrated on him; for he no longer showed himself licentious, nor did he stare madly about, but he had returned to his own self, as thoroughly as if he had been treated with drugs; and he gave up his dainty dress and summery garments and the rest of his sybaritic way of life, and he fell in love with the austerity of philosophers, and donned their cloak, and stripping off his old self modeled his life and future upon that of Apollonius. (4:20)

Resemblances to both the gospel stories of the Gerasene Demoniac (Mark 5:1-20) and the Synagogue Heckler (Mark 1:21-28) are readily apparent. The episode has many standard features of miracle stories. The stage is set, Apollonius' presence on the scene explained (cf., Mark 1:21; 5:1-2a). The demoniac draws attention to himself (cf., Mark 1:23-24; 5:2), whereupon Apollonius reveals that the trouble is supernatural, thus signaling (cf., Mark 9:19) that he is going to do something about it. Next comes the "case history": the severity of the predicament (Mark 5:3-5; 9:17-22). Apollonius adjures the demon to release his hold on his victim (cf., Mark 1:25; 5:8; 9:25), whereupon the reality of the possession is confirmed by the hysterical flailing of the demon, then the toppling of the statue as it flees (cf., Mark 5:12-13; 9:20, 26). Relieved of the demonic infestation, the former victim at once reforms his life, resolving henceforth to make Apollonius his ideal (cf., Mark 5:18). But I can't believe that, by including it, Philostratus intended to convey anything about the subject of demons and exorcisms. Isn't it far more likely that he wanted this (possibly old) story to be read allegorically as extolling philosophy as the remedy for the insolence and debauchery of youth, depicted figuratively as demon possession? Robert Bloch's story "Spawn of the Dark One"[1] is based on the same trope. Bloch writes about the plague of juvenile delinquency and motorcycle thuggery of the 1950s, "explaining" it as the fruit of liaisons between demons and women whose husbands were away fighting World War Two!

Now there was in Corinth at that time a man named Demetrius, who studied philosophy and had embraced in his system all the masculine vigor of the Cynics. Of him Favorinus in several of his works subsequently made the most generous mention, and his attitude towards Apollonius was exactly that which they say Antisthenes took up towards the system of Socrates: for he followed him and was anxious to be his disciple, and was devoted to his doctrines, and converted to the side of Apollonius the more esteemed of his own pupils. Among the latter was Menippus, a Lycian of twenty-five years of age, well endowed with good judgment, and of a physique so beautifully proportioned that in mien he resembled a fine and gentlemanly athlete. Now this Menippus was supposed by most people to be loved by a foreign woman, who was good-looking and extremely dainty, and said that she was rich; although she was really, as it turned out, not one of these things, but was only so in semblance. For as he was walking all alone along the road towards Cenchraea, he met with an apparition, and it was a woman who clasped his hand and declared that she had been long in love with him, and that she was a Phoenician woman and lived in a suburb of Corinth, and she mentioned the name of the particular suburb, and said: "When you reach the

---

1 Robert Bloch's "Spawn of the Dark One" appears in anthologies including Peter Haining, ed., *The Satanists* (New York: Pyramid Books, 1972) and *Nightmares* (New York: Belmont Books, 1961), where it appears under the alternate title "Sweet Sixteen."

place this evening, you will hear my voice as I sing to you, and you shall have wine such as you never before drank, and there will be no rival to disturb you; and we two beautiful beings will live together." The youth consented to this, for although he was in general a strenuous philosopher, he was nevertheless susceptible to the tender passion; and he visited her in the evening, and for the future constantly sought her company as his darling, for he did not yet realize that she was a mere apparition.

Then Apollonius looked over Menippus as a sculptor might do, and he sketched an outline of the youth and examined him, and having observed his foibles, he said: "You are a fine youth and are hunted by fine women, but in this case you are cherishing a serpent, and a serpent cherishes you." And when Menippus expressed his surprise, he added: "For this lady is of a kind you cannot marry. Why should you? Do you think that she loves you?" "Indeed I do," said the youth, "since she behaves to me as if she loves me." "And would you then marry her?" said Apollonius. "Why, yes, for it would be delightful to marry a woman who loves you." Thereupon Apollonius asked when the wedding was to be. "Perhaps tomorrow," said the other, "for it brooks no delay." Apollonius therefore waited for the occasion of the wedding breakfast, and then, presenting himself before the guests who had just arrived, he said: "Where is the dainty lady at whose instance ye are come?" "Here she is," replied Menippus, and at the same moment he rose slightly from his seat, blushing. "And to which of you belong the silver and gold and all the rest of the decorations of the banqueting hall?" "To the lady," replied the youth, "for this is all I have of my own," pointing to the philosopher's cloak which he wore.

And Apollonius said: "Have you heard of the gardens of Tantalus, how they exist and yet do not exist?" "Yes," they answered, "in the poems of Homer, for we certainly never went down to Hades." "As such," replied Apollonius, "you must regard this adornment, for it is not reality but the semblance of reality. And that you may realize the truth of what I say, this fine bride is one of the vampires, that is to say of those beings whom the many regard as lamias and hobgoblins. These beings fall in love, and they are devoted to the delights of Aphrodite, but especially to the flesh of human beings, and they decoy with such delights those whom they mean to devour in their feasts." And the lady said: "Cease your ill-omened talk and begone"; and she pretended to be disgusted at what she heard, and in fact she was inclined to rail at philosophers and say that they always talked nonsense. When, however, the goblets of gold and the show of silver were proved as light as air and all fluttered away out of their sight, while the wine-bearers and the cooks and all the retinue of servants vanished before the rebukes of Apollonius, the phantom pretended to weep, and prayed him not to torture her nor to compel her to confess what she really was. But Apollonius insisted and would not let her off, and then she admitted that she was a vampire, and was fattening up Menippus with pleasures before devouring his body, for it was her habit to feed upon young and beautiful bodies, because their blood is pure and strong. I have related at length, because it was necessary to do so, this the best-known story of Apollonius; for many people are aware of it and know that the incident occurred in the center of Hellas; but they have only heard in a general and vague manner that he once caught and overcame a lamia in Corinth, but they have never learned what she was about, nor that he did it to save Menippus, but I owe my own account to Damis and to the work which he wrote. (4:25)

This one is a cautionary tale for young students of philosophy, warning them to abstain from domestic and romantic entanglements. All women, it seems to say, are in effect vampires. The fine material things they cherish are mere illusions in the sense of being transitory. This one employs popular themes but does not incorporate an older, genuine miracle story. It has too much detail and narrative texture for that. If an original unit of oral tradition is deeply buried here, it has left too little evidence for us to think so.

Here too is a story which they tell of him in Tarsus. A mad dog had attacked a lad, and as a result of the bite the lad behaved exactly like a dog, for he barked and howled and went on all four feet using his hands as such, and ran about in that manner. And he had been ill in this way for thirty days, when Apollonius, who had recently come to Tarsus, met him and ordered a search to be made for the dog which had done the harm. But they said that the dog had not been found, because the youth had been attacked outside the wall when he was practicing with javelins, nor could they learn from the patient what the dog was like, for he did not even know himself any more. Then Apollonius reflected for a moment and said: "O Damis, the dog is a white shaggy sheep-dog, as big as an Amphilochian hound, and he is standing at a certain fountain trembling all over, for he is longing to drink the water, but at the same time is afraid of it. Bring him to me to the bank of the river, where there are the wrestling grounds, merely telling that it is I who call him." So Damis dragged the dog along, and it crouched at the feet of Apollonius, crying out as a suppliant might do before an altar. But he quite tamed it by stroking it with his hand, and then he stood the lad close by, holding him with his hand; and in order that the multitude might be cognizant of so great a mystery, he said: "The soul of Telephus of Mysia has been transferred into this boy, and the Fates impose the same things upon him as upon Telephus." And with these words he bade the dog lick the wound all round where he had bitten the boy, so that the agent of the wound might in turn be its physician and healer. After that the boy returned to his father and recognized his mother, and saluted his comrades as before, and drank of the waters of the Cydnus. Nor did the sage neglect the dog either, but after offering a prayer to the river he sent the dog across it; and when the dog had crossed the river, he took his stand on the opposite bank, and began to bark, a thing which mad dogs rarely do, and he folded back his ears and wagged his tail, because he knew that he was all right again, for a draught of water cures a mad dog, if he has only the courage to take it. (6:43)

This tale anticipates Stephen King's *Cujo*, sharing the premise of a dog suffering possession by the wandering soul of a dead villain. Apollonius' superhuman discernment as displayed here is really that of the omniscient narrator. It serves as an etiology, absolving the possessed of responsibility for his aberrant behavior.

PASSION AND APOTHEOSIS

Apollonius awaits his trial before Domitian, where his disciple expects he will be martyred. No, Apollonius reassures his disciple Damis,

"No one is going to kill us." "And who," said Damis, "is so invulnerable as that? But will you ever be liberated?" "So far as it rests with the verdict of the court," said Apollonius, "I shall be set at liberty this day, but so far as depends on my own will, now and here." And with these words he took his leg out of the fetters and remarked to Damis: "Here is proof positive to you of my freedom, so cheer up." Damis says that it was then for the first time that he really and truly understood the nature of Apollonius, to wit, that it was divine and superhuman, for without any sacrifice, - and how in prison could he have offered any? - and without a single prayer, without even a word, he quietly laughed at the fetters, and then inserted his leg in them afresh, and behaved like a prisoner once more. (4:44)

All right, then, Apollonius is, surely and simply, a god masquerading as a human sophist. He is only "behaving" like a prisoner, like a mortal, like a human. He is exactly like Dionysus in Euripides' *Bacchae*, in which that god appears in Thebes playing the role of the apostle of his own expanding new religion. He allows himself to be imprisoned by the blundering authorities, though, like Paul in Acts 16, he soon strolls free of his cell during an earthquake to confront his jailer. Nor is it enough to say that Philostratus' Apollonius is just like Euripides' Dionysus. We must recognize that *The Life of Apollonius of Tyana* is just like the *Bacchae*, completely a work of fiction starring a completely mythical divine protagonist.

And on the next day he called Damis and said: "My defense has to be pleaded by me on the day appointed, so do you betake yourself in the direction of Dicaearchia, for it is better to go by land; and when you have saluted Demetrius, turn aside to the sea-shore where the island of Calypso lies; for there you shall see me appear to you." "Alive," asked Damis, "or how?" Apollonius with a smile replied: "As I myself believe, alive, but as you will believe, risen from the dead." Accordingly he says that he went away with much regret, for although he did not quite despair of his master's life, yet he hardly expected him to escape death. And on the third day he arrived at Dicaearchia, where he at once heard news of the great storm which had raged during those days; for a gale with rain had burst over the sea, sinking some of the ships that were sailing thither, and driving out of their course those which were tending to Sicily and the straits of Messina. And then he understood why it was that Apollonius had bidden him to go by land. (7:41)

Apollonius warns that when Damis next sees him, he will suppose his master to have been executed and subsequently resurrected, but that he will be mistaken. Apollonius will evade death, not defeat it. Apollonius' remarks before Domitian

> aroused louder applause than beseemed the court of an Emperor; and the latter deeming the audience to have borne witness in favor of the accused, and also not a little impressed himself by the answers he had received, for they were both firm and sensible, said: "I acquit you of the charges; but you must remain here until we have had a private interview." Thereat Apollonius was much encouraged and said: "I thank you indeed, my sovereign, but I would fain tell you that by reason of these miscreants your cities are in ruin, and the islands full of exiles, and the mainland of lamentations, and your armies of cowardice, and the Senate of suspicion. Accord me also, if you will, opportunity to speak; but if not, then send someone to take my body, for my soul you cannot take. Nay, you cannot take even my body,' For thou shalt not slay me, since—I tell thee—I am not mortal.'"
>
> And with these words he vanished from the court, which was the best thing he could do under the circumstances, for the Emperor clearly intended not to question him sincerely about the case, but about all sorts of irrelevant matters. For he took great credit to himself for not having put Apollonius to death, nor was the latter anxious to be drawn into such discussions. And he thought that he would best effect his end if he left no one in ignorance of his true nature, but allowed it to be known to all to be such that he had it in him never to be taken prisoner against his own will. Moreover he had no longer any cause for anxiety about his friends; for as the despot had not the courage to ask any questions about them, how could he possibly put them to death with any color of justice upon charges for which no evidence had been presented in court? Such was the account of the proceedings of the trial which I found. (8:5)

Just before he vanishes Apollonius quotes Homer's *Iliad* (22.13) as appropriate to himself in his present circumstances. What is the original, Homeric, context? Apollonius is claiming for his own the words of Apollo speaking to Achilles. Achilles is pursuing one whom he believes to be an enemy soldier, but in fact he is chasing a disguised Apollo, who turns and, with these words, reveals his identity and, therefore, the futility of Achilles' efforts. Apollonius is taunting Domitian: he is equally impotent before one who only seemed to be a man but was actually a god. Keep in mind that Philostratus portrays Apollonius not as a demigod like Theseus and Hercules, who were exalted to godhood after death, but as a straight-up deity who merely chose to enter this world through a womb, part of the docetic charade, precisely as in the Nativity of the Buddha.

Speaking of Homer, in chapter 16 Apollonius repeats Odysseus' pilgrimage to the tomb of Achilles. He calls out, like Jesus to Lazarus,

> "O Achilles, ... most of mankind declare you are dead, but I cannot agree with them... show... yourself to my eyes, if you should be able to use them to attest your existence." Thereupon a slight earthquake shook the neighborhood of the barrow [cf. Matthew 28:1-2], and a youth issued forth five cubits high, wearing a cloak of Thessalian fashion... but he grew bigger, till he was twice as large and even more than that; at any rate he appeared .. to be twelve cubits high just at that moment when he reached his complete stature, and his beauty grew apace with his length. (4:15)

How, I ask you, is this any different from Odysseus seeking out Achilles in Hades? We are reading fiction in both cases, the one story probably a conscious imitation of the other. Is there any more reason for us to posit a historical Apollonius than a historical Odysseus?

> Damis' grief had just broken out afresh, and he had made some such exclamation as the following: "Shall we ever behold, O ye gods, our noble and good companion?" when Apollonius, who had heard him—for as a matter of fact he was already present in the chamber of the nymphs—answered: "Ye shall see him, nay, ye have already seen him." "Alive?" said Demetrius, "For if you are dead, we have anyhow never ceased to lament you." Hereupon Apollonius stretched out his hand and said: "Take hold of me, and if I evade you, then I am indeed a ghost come to you from the realm of Persephone, such as the gods of the underworld reveal to those who are dejected with much mourning. But if I resist your touch,

then you shall persuade Damis also that I am both alive and that I have not abandoned my body." They were no longer able to disbelieve, but rose up and threw themselves on his neck and kissed him, and asked him about his defense. For while Demetrius was of opinion that he had not even made his defense—for he expected him to be destroyed without any wrong being proved against him—Damis thought that he had made his defense, but perhaps more quickly than was expected; for he never dreamed that he had made it only that day. But Apollonius said: "I have made my defense, gentlemen, and have gained my cause; and my defense took place this very day not so long ago, for it lasted on even to midday." "How then," said Demetrius, "have you accomplished so long a journey in so small a fraction of the day?" And Apollonius replied: "Imagine what you will, flying ram or wings of wax excepted, so long as you ascribe it to the intervention of a divine escort." (8:12)

The memoirs then of Apollonius of Tyana which Damis the Assyrian composed, end with the above story; for with regard to the manner in which he died, if he did actually die, there are many stories. (8:29)

Now there are some who relate that he died in Ephesus [...] Others again say that he (Apollonius) died in Lindus, where he entered the temple of Athene and disappeared within it. Others again say that he died in Crete in a much more remarkable manner than the people of Lindus relate. For they say that he continued to live in Crete, where he became a greater centre of admiration than ever before, and that he came to the temple of Dictynna late at night. Now this temple is guarded by dogs, whose duty is to watch over the wealth deposited in it, and the Cretans claim that they are as good as bears or any other animals equally fierce. Nonetheless, when he came, instead of barking, they approached him and fawned upon him, as they would not have done even with people they knew familiarly. The guardians of the shrine arrested him in consequence, and threw him in bonds as a wizard and a robber, accusing him of having thrown to the dogs some charmed morsel. But about midnight he loosened his bonds, and after calling those who had bound him, in order that they might witness the spectacle, he ran to the doors of the temple, which opened wide to receive him; and when he had passed within they closed afresh. as they had been shut, and there was heard a chorus of maidens singing from within the temple, and their song was this. "Hasten thou from earth, hasten thou to Heaven, hasten." In other words: "Do thou go upwards from earth." (8:30)

It is by no means hard to guess which of these reports Philostratus prefers. For him, for the sake of his story, Apollonius did not die because, like his namesake Apollo, he *could* not die, being an immortal god. He simply hops aboard the celestial elevator and returns to Olympus. This is not an adoptionistic exaltation. He is simply a god returning to heaven. And who's to say he cannot make occasional descents from there?

> There came to Tyana a youth who did not shrink from acrimonious discussions, and who would not accept truth in argument. Now Apollonius had already passed away from among men, but people still wondered at his passing, and no one ventured to dispute that he was immortal. This being so, the discussions were mainly about the soul, for a band of youths were there passionately addicted to wisdom. The young man in question, however, would on no account allow the tenet of the immortality of the soul, and said: "I myself, gentlemen, have done nothing now for nine months but pray to Apollonius that he would reveal to me the truth about the soul; but he is so utterly dead that he will not appear to me in response to my entreaties, nor give me any reason to consider him immortal." Such were the young man's words on that occasion, but on the fifth day following, after discussing the same subject, he fell asleep where he was talking with them, and of the young men who were studying with him, some were reading books, and others were industriously drawing geometrical figures on the ground, when on a sudden, like one possessed, he leaped up still in a half sleep, streaming with perspiration, and cried out: "I believe thee." And, when those who were present asked him what was the matter; "Do you not see," said he, "Apollonius the sage, how that he is present with us and is listening to our discussion, and is reciting wondrous verses about the soul?" "But where is he?" they asked, "For we cannot see him anywhere, although we would rather do so than possess all the blessings of mankind." And the youth replied: "It would seem that he is come to converse with myself alone concerning the tenets which I would not believe." (8:31)

This episode is strikingly parallel to the "Doubting Thomas" story in John chapter 20, offering readers a vicarious "eyewitness" experience of Apollonius. But don't get excited; you *still* haven't seen him. But there is an even more significant implication: anyone ever saw Apollonius only in private visions, i.e., with the eye of faith, the same way Aelius Aristides "saw" Asclepius and Serapis—in dreams and visions. I should think that belief in the divine healer Asclepius began with dreams in his temples, which in turn led to the stories (myths) of a previous historical existence of this son of Apollo on earth. In like manner, I think "Apolloniusism" began with dreams and trance visions like the one quoted just above, subjective apparitions of the god Proteus-Apollonius, with the notion of his earthly ministry following later. And stories is all they ever were. No, Virginia, there was no historical Apollonius of Tyana.

William Lane Craig: Scholar or Apologist?

Dr. Craig often appeals to the consensus of New Testament scholars on behalf of conservative views. By contrast, I am glad to confess that the opinion of the majority of scholars makes no difference whatever to me. In fact, in the Gospels, after all, it's the consensus of scholars in the Sanhedrin that condemns Jesus to death. As Francis Schaeffer used to say, "You can't settle the question of truth by majority vote." I think Martin Luther and Galileo and others knew that, too.

If I am interested in a question, I must examine the issues for myself. I reject, for example, Velikovsky's astronomy, not because the academy sneers at it, which I guess they do, but because his methodology seems flawed to me, as I understand it. And forgive me, but so does Dr. Craig's.

First, let me call attention to two fundamental axioms of Dr. Craig's work. The first is what strikes me as a kind of double-truth model. The second is the old red-herring attempt to evade the principle of historical analogy, by means of the claim that critics reject miracle stories only because they espouse philosophical naturalism. The second follows from the first, and both commit the fallacy of ad hominem argumentation, even while projecting it onto the opponent.

I think he tips his hand at the end of the first chapter of his book *Reasonable Faith*. He draws a distinction there between *knowing* Christianity is true and *showing* that it is true. He says,

"What, then, should be our approach in apologetics? It should be something like this: 'My friend, I know Christianity is true because God's Spirit lives in me and assures me that it is true, and you can know it too because God is knocking at the door of your heart, telling you the same thing. If you are sincerely seeking God, then God will give you assurance that the Gospel is true. Now, to show you it's true, I'll share with you some arguments and evidence that I really find convincing. But should my argument seem weak and unconvincing to you, that's my fault, not God's. It only shows that I'm a poor apologist, not that the Gospel is untrue. Whatever you think of my arguments, God still loves you and holds you accountable. I'll do my best to present good arguments to you, but ultimately you have to deal not with arguments, but with God himself.'" (page 48)

A little further on, he saith,

"Unbelief is at the root a spiritual, not an intellectual, problem. Sometimes an unbeliever will throw up an intellectual smokescreen so that he can avoid personal, existential involvement with the Gospel." (pages 49-50)

Dr. Craig then freely admits his conviction arises from purely subjective factors. To me, it sounds no different in principle from the teenage Mormon doorknocker. He tells you he knows the Book of Mormon was written by ancient Americans because he has a warm, swelling feeling inside when he asks God if it's true.

Certain intellectual questions have to receive certain answers, then, to be consistent with this revivalistic, heartwarming experience, so Dr. Craig knows in advance, for example, that Strauss and Bultmann must have been wrong, and by hook or by crook he'll find a way to get from here to there. His enterprise is circular, since he grounds Christian belief upon a subjective state described already in Christian theological terminology: God's Spirit dwelling in his heart, etc.

Dr. Craig seems to admit that he holds his faith on purely subjective grounds, but maintains that he's lucky to discover that the facts, objectively considered, happen to bear out his faith. Whereas, theoretically, his faith might not prove true to the facts, in actually—whew!—it does. In any case, it's obvious from the same quotes that the arguments are ultimately beside the point. If an unbeliever doesn't see the cogency of Dr. Craig's brand of New Testament criticism, the same thing exactly as his apologetics, it can only be because the doubter has some guilty secret to hide and doesn't want to repent and let Jesus run his life. If one sincerely seeks God, Dr. Craig's arguments will mysteriously start looking pretty good to him.

Dr. Craig's frank expression to his fellow evangelists and apologists is quite revealing. He tells you to say to the unbeliever that you find these arguments really convincing, but how can Dr. Craig simply take this for granted unless, as I'm sure he does, he knows he is writing to people for whom the cogency of the arguments is a foregone conclusion. They're arguments in behalf of a position his readers are already committed to as an *a priori* party line.

His is a position that exalts voluntaristic decision above rational deliberation. Rational deliberation, though good, is by itself not good enough for the evangelist because it can never justify a quick decision, such as Campus Crusades' booklet "The Four Spiritual Laws" solicits. Every one of Dr. Craig's scholarly articles on the resurrection implicitly ends with that little decision card for the reader to sign to invite Jesus into his heart as his personal savior. He's not trying to do disinterested historical or exegetical research; he's trying to get folks saved. I know the feeling. I used to be the president of an Inter-Varsity chapter.

Note how he characterizes people who do not accept his version of the historical Jesus as "unbelievers" who merely cast up "smoke-screens" of insincere carping. But this functions as a mirror image of his own enterprise. His apparently self-effacing pose—"If my arguments fail to convince, then I must have done a poor job of explaining them"—just reveals the whole exercise to be a sham. The arguments are offered cynically, whatever it takes. If they don't work, take your pick between brimstone—"God holds you accountable"—and treacle—"God still loves you."

I'm not saying Dr. Craig is wittingly distorting the truth to win his point; obviously he's not. But he is so committed to a dogmatic party line that he cannot see truth as meaning anything but that party line. In Dr. Craig's lexicon, you look up truth, and it says, "See 'Gospel.'" To borrow Francis Schaeffer's terminology again, for the apologist, truth becomes merely a connotation word. Just as liberal theologian Albrecht Ritschl said, "Jesus has the value of God for us," the apologist might say, "Christianity has the value of truth for us." Just as William James said that righteous endeavor was the moral equivalent of war, for apologists, Christianity is the moral equivalent of truth.

Only it doesn't work. For Ritschlianism, Jesus was in fact not God. For William James, moral endeavor was not in fact war. Even so, anything that substitutes for the truth may be preferred to the truth, but then it's a fiction.

If the charge that unbelievers are hiding behind a smokescreen is a mirror image of the apologist's own strategy, then the "naturalistic presuppositions" business is a specific instance of such childish "I know you are, but what am I?" tactics. Does it take a blanket presupposition for an historian to discount some miracle stories, like Elisha's axe head on the one extreme or the resurrection of Jesus on the other, as legendary? No, because as Bultmann recognized, there is no problem accepting reports even of extraordinary things that we can verify as still occurring today, like faith healings and exorcisms. However you may wish to account for them, you can go to certain meetings and see scenes resembling those in the Gospels, so it is by no means a matter of rejecting all miracle stories on principle.

Biblical critics are not like Carl Sagan or James Randi, going into every investigation already convinced that the paranormal must be a fraud. No, they take miracle stories on a case-by-case basis. But such a selective, piecemeal, and probabilistic acceptance of miracle stories is not what apologists want. They take umbrage that biblical critics do not wind up accepting *any and all* biblical miracles. So, if it would not require a blanket principle to *reject* the historicity of particular miracle stories, we must ask if it would take a blanket principle to *require acceptance* of all biblical miracles. Clearly, it would, and that principle cannot be mere supernaturalism, that is, openness to the possibility that miracles can occur. One can believe God capable of anything without believing that he actually did everything anybody may say he did. One can believe in the possibility of miracles without believing that every reported miracle must have occurred. No, the requisite principle for accepting all biblical miracles is the principle of biblical inerrancy, the belief that all biblical narratives are historically accurate simply because they appear in the Bible. After all, it will not greatly upset Dr. Craig any more than it upset Warfield to deny the historical accuracy of medieval reports of miracles wrought by the Virgin Mary or the sacramental wafer, much less stories of miracles wrought by Gautama Buddha or Apollonius of Tyana.

Supernaturalism is not at all the issue here. The issue is whether the historian is to abdicate his role as a sifter of evidence by accepting the dogma of inerrancy, even if clandestinely. I know Dr. Craig says he is sticking only to the elements of the Gospel story accepted as historical by most scholars, but this is only tactical. He's shortening the apologetical line of defense. Once he has you in the fold, he'll press on to full inerrantism.

Nor is naturalism the issue when the historian employs the principle of analogy. As F.H. Bradley showed in *The Presuppositions of Critical History*, no historical inference is possible unless the historian assumes a basic analogy of past experience with present experience. If we do not grant this, nothing will seem amiss in believing stories that A turned into a werewolf or B changed lead into gold. "Hey, just because we don't see it happening today doesn't prove it never did!" One could just as easily accept the historicity of Jack and the Beanstalk on the same basis as long as one's sole criterion for historical plausibility is "Anything goes." If there are ancient parallel legends about other saviors and sages rising from death or ascending into heaven, but there is no present-day instance, is the historian to be maligned as a narrow dogmatist or a moral coward refusing to repent if he judges the story of Jesus' resurrection as probably a legend, too?

The historical axiom of analogy does not dogmatize. Critical historians are not engaging in metaphysics and epistemology as if they could hop into a time machine and pontificate, "A didn't happen, B did!" Again, Dr. Craig and his brethren are just projecting. It is they and not critical historians who want to be able to point to sure results. Imagine a creed: "If thou shalt confess with thy mouth the Lord Jesus and believe in thy heart that God hath probably raised him from the dead, thou shalt most likely be saved." Now, who's the joke on there? Historians don't have creeds. They frame hypotheses. Sure, you can find some hidebound prof, some small-minded, insecure windbag who will not budge from a pet theory because he has too much personally invested in it, but you have no trouble recognizing such a person as a hack, a fake, a bad historian who ought to know better: Holocaust deniers, for example. The last thing you do is to emulate such behavior and make it into an operating principle. But apologists do; again, it's projection.

It reduces to this: At the end of the "Four Spiritual Laws" booklet, there's a cartoon diagram showing a toy locomotive engine labeled "Fact" pulling a coal car labelled "Faith," followed in turn by a superfluous caboose tagged "Feeling." The new convert is admonished to let faith rest on fact, not to allow faith to waver with feelings. But one must suspect that it is the caboose that is pulling the train, and pulling it backward. Faith is based "firmly" on *feeling*, and certain notions are postulated as fact and defended as such because of the security they afford the sick soul who seeks a port in the existential storm.

Dr. Craig has had occasion to cross swords with John Dominic Crossan. One need not agree with Crossan—I seldom do—to appreciate that he is however an innovative and creative New Testament scholar, that he marshals his vast learning in an attempt to find out new things from the Gospels. Crossan is concerned to advance the state of knowledge; contrast him with Dr. Craig who uses his own formidable erudition in one vast damage control operation. Every effort of Dr. Craig's is to squelch new theories that threaten to cast doubt on the traditional picture of the storybook Jesus. One feels that Dr. Craig would sooner put his efforts elsewhere than putting out fires lit by Bultmann, Strauss, and Crossan. If he had his way, he'd be occupied with something more edifying; at least that's the feeling I get.

Evangelicals think they've got the truth in their back pocket, so they can't be trying to find what they think they've already got. Novelty is the devil. They expend great time and efforts mastering the skills of Greek and Hebrew exegesis. Witness the unparalleled excellence of Dallas Theological Seminary in these areas. But for what? All their efforts at exegesis are the laborings of a mountain to bring forth a mouse. If one of them really comes up with something new theologically, it will result in immediate charges of heresy. The effort is solely to hold the fort against the advance of intellectual history.

Dr. Craig everywhere presupposes a pre-critical picture of the Gospels as straightforward records of reporting, without tendential bias. He tries to make the Markan empty tomb tale a piece of sober contemporary history. We're told that the story is unvarnished history, since it betrays no signs of theological tendency. No theological coloring? In a story told to attest the resurrection of the Son of God from the dead? What else *is* it? Isn't it *all* varnish, Formica instead of wood?

Charles Talbert (by the way, no God-hating atheist, but a Southern Baptist), in his book *What Is a Gospel?* has no trouble adducing abundant parallels from Hellenistic hero biographies, in which the ascensions into heaven of Romulus, Aeneas, Hercules, Aristaeus, Empedocles, Apollonius, etc., are inferred from the utter failure of their searching disciples to find any vestige of their bones, bodies, or clothing where they might be expected to be found. Sometimes, they make a postmortem appearance to their grieving and worshipful followers. These stories, like all ancient miracle tales, include the element of initial skepticism by the disciples, who are then convinced despite themselves. It's just a narrative device. None of them are factual reports.

Talbert concludes that the empty tomb and resurrection stories in the Gospels would have been familiar genres to ancient readers, as of course they were. Pagan critics hastened to point out the similarities, and Christian apologists lamely countered that Satan had counterfeited the Gospel episodes in advance to throw unbelievers off the track.

Contra Dr. Craig, the empty tomb story is theological through and through. If we're truly interested in history, how can we dismiss other ancient "vanished body and postmortem appearance" stories, making an exception in the single case of Jesus who just happens to be the founder of our religion? And once we recognize the Gospel resurrection narratives to be cut from the same cloth, all questions of whether the women went to the wrong tomb, or if the disciples stole the body (or borrowed it or whatever!), or whether the Sanhedrin could have produced it with dental records to prove who it was, or whether the disciples saw hallucinations, or a case of mistaken identity, it's all seen to be moot.

THE END

WEIRD WEBZINE
FANTASY & SURREALITY